NATURE BOUND
POCKET FIELD GUIDE

NATURE BOUND
Pocket Field Guide

by Ron Dawson

OMNIgraphics Ltd.
Boise, Idaho

NATURE BOUND

International Standard Book Number (ISBN): 0-9609776-7-8
Library of Congress Catalog Number: 84-62841

Copyright © 1985 by OMNIgraphics Ltd.
Boise, Idaho 83702

Printed in Canada.

To him

who in the love
of Nature holds
Communion with her
visible forms,

she speaks . . .

Opening lines from THANATOPSIS
— William Cullen Bryant

ACKNOWLEDGMENTS

Plant Verification

La Rea D. Johnston, Ph.D.
Oregon State University Herbarium

Amy Jean Gilmartin, Ph.D.
Joy Mastrogiuseppe
Assistant Curator
Marion Ownbey Herbarium
Washington State University

Plant Toxicology

Steven J. Gill, Ph.D.
Washington State University

First Aid
written in consultation with

Glenn C. Bothwell, M.D.
Eagle, Idaho

J. Robert Polk, M.D.
Boise, Idaho

Technical Review

USAF Survival School
Fairchild AFB, Washington
Col. Norm A. McDaniel, Commander

FOREWORD

The vast North American wilderness, encroached upon and subjugated by man, is retreating. The increase in population alone over the past one hundred and fifty years has turned once beautiful valleys into huge metropolitan complexes; virgin forests into massive logging operations; and rivers, lakes and mountains into giant hydroelectric projects, resorts and ski areas.

It is not, however, our intent to label or find fault, nor even to debate the pros and cons of these changes. After all, even the paper on which this is printed was once a tree, the press upon which this book is printed is powered by a hydroelectric facility; and it all happened in a major metropolitan complex in North America.

The fact is, with all that man has done or failed to do, there yet remain vast wilderness areas which, if not inaccessible, are nearly so. And because man, with his spirit of adventure, travel and exploration, ventures into these wilderness regions, the need exists to educate him, not only to survive if need be, but to plant within him the seeds of respect, appreciation and understanding for that which remains. Protecting the remaining wilderness then, is a function of man's attitude while both in and apart from it. In either case, whether as a guest of its manifold beauty or a user of its untold resource, one ought not offend or abuse the host and provider.

To this end we dedicate this handbook of wilderness appreciation and wilderness survival.

Special Acknowledgments

Marjorie C. Bue, winner of numerous journalistic awards, for her extraordinary editing and proofing skill that honed and polished a rugged manuscript into a work of professional excellence.

Pamela Harper, for allowing us to use three slides from her collection *(Atropa belladona, Gelsemium sempervirens,* and *Rhus vernex).*

Robert Landsburg (killed in the 1980 Mount St. Helens eruption), who assisted the author with the plant photography.

CONTENTS

INTRODUCTION

The term "survival" for our purposes will be defined as emergency living under primitive or semi-primitive conditions in a wilderness environment. The word "survivalist," although not found in the dictionary, is our term for one who is in the process or the act of surviving — within the context of our previous definition of the word survival.

The intent and scope of this manual is to facilitate and insure survival under a variety of wilderness conditions throughout North America. Specifically, this manual deals with the knowledge, skills, equipment and environmental resources which will provide for human adaptation and survival in frequently unfamiliar and sometimes hostile environments, **usually under emergency conditions.**

In this presentation we will address human adaptation in terms of the five basic needs required in survival: water, food, heat (warmth), shelter, and the spiritual or psychological needs. Although we tend to apply these terms in the formula of wilderness survival, they are the essence of survival in any environment. The order of acquisition of the basic five may vary depending upon physiological need; however, subtract any two — or even one under some circumstances — and the result will likely be non-survival.

The knowledge that nature is neither for nor against one is primary to coping with the unfamiliar environment and controlling the emotion of fear. Because the survival situation is generally brought about by an initially unrelated emergency and compounded by unfamiliar surroundings or even an injury, the instinctive reaction is to magnify the circumstances. The resulting fear weakens the ability to think and plan. However, we should keep in mind that although we may be unable to control the circumstance, we can to a large extent control how we operate and live within it.

Helping to put the circumstances in workable perspective is the secondary aim of this manual. Read and understand its contents in advance of the need to use them. The matter-of-fact treatment of the various subjects should instill the confidence that one will be able to survive.

We cannot guarantee the survivalist will encounter any emergency without some fear, but we can guarantee he will be equipped with the knowledge to thoughtfully deal with most of the pressing problems of his survival.

What this manual cannot teach is the will to live, and in the last analysis the will to live is the most important ingredient in survival. Knowledge and equipment without the will to live are of little value. There are many recorded survival encounters wherein the will to live, alone, was the deciding factor.

IMMEDIATE ACTION

Emergency situations are rarely the same and the priority of the immediate action to be taken will obviously vary. The order in which you set your priorities will largely depend on the immediate environment and your physical and mental state. Take the time to appraise your circumstances in light of your physical condition and the resources that are available. Every decision in a survival situation is important. In short, **think before you act** and **conserve your strength**.

The following list will help you to establish the priorities:

1. **Treat injuries, if any.**
2. **If it is late in the day, fire and shelter will be your first concerns.**
3. **In desert area, set up one or more solar stills.**
4. **Gather adequate fuel for the first night.**
5. **Lay out signal fires and/or signal patterns and have ready other signaling devices.**
6. **Set traps and snares.**
7. **Reevaluate your circumstances.**

Assume that you are going to spend several days. Resist the urge to feel sorry for yourself and concentrate on making your stay as tolerable as possible. This possibly sounds easier than it is, but consider the alternative. Survival is not by chance; it is by discipline — a discipline of attitude, thought and action.

FIRE

The importance of knowing how to start and maintain a fire can be readily appreciated by the following impressive, although highly generalized, survival data under winter conditions:

Human expiration without food — 30 days
Human expiration without water — 6 days
Human expiration without heat — 24 hours

Fire then, under most survival conditions, is the first priority. However, producing fire can be most difficult, and the wetter and colder the conditions, the more difficult it becomes to produce.

The prospect of starting a fire without matches is not usually a pleasant one. Fire by friction depends on just the right kind of wood, which has to be bone dry. The flint and steel method requires some type of hard stone such as flint, obsidian, quartzite or agate and something which the spark will ignite. The most reliable tinder for this method is charred cloth or fine steel wool, neither of which is usually available when the fire is needed. A magnifying glass or the reflector from an automobile headlight or aircraft landing light both require sunlight, dry tinder and patience. The point being made here is that **if you are going to resort to fire by friction, it is highly desirable that one of the sticks be a match.** Matches have earned an enviable reputation in the field of fire making and should be carried in a waterproof container and on your person at all times. The strike-anywhere type match is best.

Having matches however, doesn't necessarily mean that you are going to have a fire. You still need dry tinder, kindling, fuel and a certain amount of skill. The instructions given here are for starting a fire under difficult circmstances.

1. **Select a sheltered area** if possible.
    a. If raining — select a spot under a tree or rock ledge.
    b. If ground is snow-covered, prepare a fire platform, heat reflector and kindling bar (13.1) of green logs.
2. **Select tinder material which will readily ignite.** Dry paper (i.e., tear non-

13.1 Fire Platform & Heat Reflector

13.2 Teepee / Candle Fire Start

essental pages from this field guide such as contents, bibliography, etc.), pitch, small brittle dead limbs called "squaw wood" found near the base of coniferous (evergreen) trees are all excellent tinder materials. With a knife cut away wet bark or wet surface to cut dry slivers and wood chips. In wet weather the most available tinder is usually the tiny brittle branchlets from dead limbs. These should be no larger than the diameter of a pencil lead since they will burn even when damp. Select the ones that snap when broken.

3. **Protect tinder and kindling materials** from moisture until you have gathered ample fire building ingredients. Put them in your pocket, pack or plastic bag.

4. When an **ample supply of tinder, kindling and fuel** has been gathered, carefully arrange the tinder with the most flammable or easily ignited on the bottom and the next above, etc. (i.e., paper, dry shavings, tiny squaw wood twigs, larger squaw wood and so on). Build a small pile in the shape of a tee-pee (13.2) three or four inches high. If pitch (which is not affected by moisture) or fire start tablets are available, either may be used at or near the base of the tinder.

5. **Protect the match** during ignition using cupped hands and body to block wind and rain. Set lighted match to candle wick and then place the still burning match in tinder. The match may ignite the tinder; if it doesn't, the lighted candle offers a second chance without expending another match.

6. When using the **candle to light the tinder,** hold it at the least downward wick angle to prevent melting wax from running down the wick and extinguishing the flame. Allow candle to burn for a few minutes until you are assured of a successful fire building attempt.

7. **Blow lightly** on the burning wood. This helps increase the flame and the intensity of the heat.

8. **Fire climbs,** so always add new kindling above the flame. Add additional squaw wood and kindling material as the flame increases, being careful not to overwhelm and smother the fire. Soft woods make the best kindling; split branches burn faster than whole ones.

9. **Store wet and damp fuel near fire** to permit some drying before use.
10. **Small fires are easier to control;** they use less fuel and their heat can be concentrated.

Fortunately, in dry weather there is frequently a greater selection of tinder materials, including pine needles, grasses, certain mosses, cattails, sagebrush, bark, etc., and the fire building chore is made easier.

In order to obtain the most warmth and at the same time protect the fire from the effect of the wind, build it against a rock or wall of logs (13.1, 17.1). This will serve as a reflector to direct the heat into your shelter.

To make a fire last overnight, place two or three large logs over it. When the fire has burned well into them and a good bed of coals has been formed, cover it lightly with ashes and then dry earth. This banked fire will still be smoldering in the morning. **It is much easier to keep a fire going than it is to rekindle one,** especially in a wet environment.

With your first fire you should char some cloth by burning it without air in a closed container such as a coffee can or by enwrapping the cloth in a ball of clay and firing it until scorching occurs. Use this charred cloth for tinder to catch the spark from flint and steel. Your knife and the flint on the bottom of the waterproof match box will generate a good spark. When the spark catches and the cloth glows red, place it quickly in some tinder and blow into a flame.

We will not go into several other methods of fire starting for the simple reason that most of them are only applicable when the most desirable conditions prevail.

SHELTER

In the previous chapter we mentioned the importance of fire and its by-product heat. This alone, however, may not be enough. One cold, windy, rainy night spent in the open with a fire, but without a shelter, is devastating to the morale, if not to the physical well-being.

The type of shelter you construct will depend on the season, materials available, time of day, your physical condition, and your ingenuity.

1. **Shelter Site Selection** — Does it offer?
    a. Protection from the wind, flash floods, avalanche, etc.
    b. Protection from plant, reptile and insect pests (i.e., poison oak, rattle snakes, mosquitoes).
    c. Ample shelter-making and bed-making material.
    d. Availability of drinking water.
    e. Availability of adequate fuel for fire.
    f. Suitable amount of level ground for a fairly comfortable bed.
2. **Shelter Type Selection** — Will it be?
    a. Protective enough for the conditions. (Will it keep you dry and protect you from the wind?)
    b. Large enough to permit a bed, equipment and fuel storage.
    c. Strong enough to withstand wind and snow, if these are factors.
    d. Used in conjunction with a fire.
    e. Used for one or several days.

Construction information and techniques for several wilderness shelters follow:

"A" Frame Lean-to:

This is an excellent simple shelter which can be easily constructed with boughs or a plastic sheet or tarp (17.1, 18.2). It will accommodate one or two persons. The ridge pole should be about 12 feet long, supported by two forked sticks, the ends of which are driven into the ground six or seven feet apart. The forks of these sticks

17.1 Bough "A Frame" Construction

should come together to support the ridge pole about five feet above the ground (18.1). If plastic or tarp is available, place it over the framework, allowing excess plastic to be folded inside to provide a ground cloth. Place rocks or pole sections along the two inside walls to keep the walls taut. Boughs may be placed over the plastic to help hold it in place and provide additional insulation. Of course, in the absence of plastic or in the event of it being used for a solar still, the entire shelter can be made from boughs and bark. Boughs and/or bark should be placed in shingle fashion, working from the bottom up.

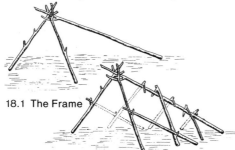

18.1 The Frame

18.2 The Cover

Wickiup:
   The wickiup was a shelter used by the nomadic Indians of the arid regions of the western and southwestern United States. This shelter contains three or more sturdy ridge poles as the supporting members, arranged in the shape of a cone or teepee. This rough frame is then covered with a variety of available materials including reed grass, brushwood, pine or fir boughs, moss, bark, etc. The length of the supporting poles and the circumference at which they are set dictate the height and size of the wickiup. Fifteen-foot-long poles will make a nine or ten foot diameter living area which is adequate for four people.

19.1 Snow Cave (cross section)

Snow Cave:

Snow is an excellent insulating material. A cubic foot of snow is a mass of tiny air pockets which, in effect, provide a kind of super insulation.

The snow cave (19.1) is the finest of all emergency winter shelters. It can be dug with an improvised snow shovel (i.e. frying pan, snowshoe, or even with the hands). If possible select a site where the snow has drifted. In snow-covered forested areas the cave entrance should be dug in the depression about the base of a large tree.

Throughout the construction, work slowly and take frequent rests to avoid overheating. Perspiration-soaked clothing, once your work has stopped, will provide little comfort.

To construct the cave entrance dig in and slightly down. Then dig up 18 to 20 inches above the entry to make the bed platform. This platform should be insulated with evergreen boughs, bark or any other material available to keep your body from direct contact with the snow. The snow cave wall should be a minimum of 18″ in thickness. Punch a ventilation hole in the roof and keep it open by poking a stick up through it occasionally. The doorway should not be closed off completely. Leave a small opening to insure fresh air circulation. A lighted candle will provide additional heat as well as light.

The temperature inside a small, well-constructed snow cave, warmed by your body heat alone, will be 10 degrees or more above the outside temperature. Although the size and construction may be cause for variations in the following example, it does graphically illustrate the value of the snow cave. Example: If the outside temperature is zero degrees F. with a wind of 40 miles per hour (21.1) you can expect:

Outside with no protection . . .

minus 55 degrees F. windchill* factor (exposed flesh may freeze in one minute).
Inside the snow cave . . .

no windchill; temperature inside increased by 10 degrees or more within a few minutes.
Inside the snow cave with a lighted candle . . .

temperatures inside increases an additional 10 to 20 degrees.

In this situation it was possible to alter the temperature/windchill effect by 75 to 85 degrees by elimination of the windchill factor and the increase of the base temperature (zero degrees F.) by 20 to 30 degrees. Although it is possible to bring the inside temperature above 32 degrees F., it is not recommended for obvious reasons.

---

*Windchill: a combination of temperature and wind speed that would have the same effect on exposed human flesh as a given still-air temperature.

TEMPERATURE & WINDCHILL CHART

WIND SPEED		COOLING POWER OF WIND EXPRESSED AS "EQUIVALENT CHILL TEMPERATURE"									
KNOTS	MPH	TEMPERATURE (F)									
CALM	CALM	40	30	20	10	0	-10	-20	-30	-40	-50	-60

		EQUIVALENT CHILL TEMPERATURE									
3 - 6	5	35	25	15	5	-5	-15	-25	-35	-45	-55	-70
7 - 10	10	30	15	5	-10	-20	-35	-45	-60	-70	-80	-95
11 - 15	15	25	10	-5	-20	-30	-45	-60	-70	-85	-100	-110
16 - 19	20	20	5	-10	-25	-35	-50	-65	-80	-95	-110	-120
20 - 23	25	15	0	-15	-30	-45	-60	-75	-90	-105	-120	-135
24 - 28	30	10	0	-20	-30	-50	-65	-80	-95	-110	-125	-140
29 - 32	35	10	-5	-20	-35	-50	-65	-80	-100	-115	-130	-145
33 - 36	40	10	-5	-20	-35	-55	-70	-85	-100	-115	-130	-150

WINDS ABOVE 40 HAVE LITTLE ADDITIONAL EFFECT	LITTLE DANGER	INCREASING DANGER (Flesh may freeze within 1 minute)	GREAT DANGER (Flesh may freeze within 30 seconds)

21.1 Temperature / Windchill Chart

Remember to keep the vent hole open and take your snow-digging tool into the shelter at night in the event you have to dig out after a storm.

Snow Trench:

If wind packed or wet packed snow is available the snow trench shelter (22.1) will provide protection from the chilling effects of the wind and can be constructed in a relatively short period of time. This shelter should be considered when it is late in the day and darkness is approaching.

A trench about three feet wide and a little longer than your body is adequate. Cut the blocks for the roof about six inches thick and lay them aside as you remove them from the trench. These are then leaned against each other to form the roof. The trench should be just deep enough so that you can sit up without bumping your head. The last end block is pulled into place from the inside. The bed (floor) of this shelter is prepared in the same manner as that of the snow cave and is further described below in the description of the bough bed. Scoop out a shelf on one side for your candle. A

22.1 Snow Trench

single candle in this small shelter will soon provide enough heat for comfort. Incidentally, the life of a plumber's type candle (approximately ¾ inch diameter by 5½ inches in length) is four hours, an important consideration when designing a survival kit for snow country application.

Construction of a Bough Bed:

An evergreen bough bed will insulate you from the ground cold and dampness. Take special care in constructing the bough bed. Because your activity will be limited after dark and because of your need to conserve energy, you will be spending more time than usual lying. Therefore, the time and effort spent in making this bed may mean the difference between a reasonable night and a miserable night. Select boughs from ground level and work around the tree. Cut them no larger than a common lead pencil. Gather enough to make a bed at least ten inches deep. Start by placing a small log across the front of the shelter (not necessary in the case of a snow shelter). Against this log arrange the fir boughs in rows with the cut off ends to the ground and the tip ends toward you. Evergreen boughs have a natural curve and the convex side of this curve should be up to give the bed springiness. Continue the rows laid shingle-fashion until the desired length is reached. Extra boughs can be added where necessary after giving the bed the comfort test. Lots of boughs mean better insulation from the ground and more comfort.

WATER

About **80 percent of your body is water,** and your vital life processes center around the balance of intake versus output of this important element. Every bit of body water is needed for normal functioning, and when loss of water exceeds intake, dehydration results and the body pays for this loss by reduced efficency. Dehydration of six to ten percent of the body weight will result in the following symptoms in the order listed: dizziness, headache, difficulty in breathing, tingling in arms and legs, and a dry mouth. The body becomes bluish, speech is indistinct and finally the person is unable to walk. Unless water is made available, death soon follows. However, an individual who has collapsed from dehydration can be revived in a few minutes by gradually replacing his lost water. Ten percent dehydration will not result in any permanent physical damage providing water is replaced within several hours.

Normally, an adult male exchanges about three quarts of water a day. One and one-half quarts is lost as urine in carrying off metabolic wastes. About one half quart is lost through the lungs in humidifying the air that we breathe. The other half quart is lost through the evaporation of insensible perspiration in the process of cooling the body and keeping its temperature at 98.6 degrees F. These requirements can change dramatically depending on the weather and physical activity. The body absorbs heat from the air as well as radiant heat from the sun and any kind of work or exercise produces body heat. This excess heat must be dissipated and this is accomplished by the evaporation of perspiration on the surface of the skin. **Therefore, for the survivalist whose supply of water is limited, the problem becomes one of rationing water losses rather than rationing water intake.** You should drink available water until your thirst is satisfied instead of rationing it in an attempt to stretch the supply. Concentrate on conserving the water in your body by reducing the body's basic needs for water.

Since urine accounts for the largest loss of water, this is a good place to start. Here water serves as a solvent or "carrier" for chemical by-products or wastes of body metabolism (the conversion of food into usable energy and into tissue for repair or storage). These are metabolized when necessary to provide energy. Thus, by decreasing the amount of food eaten (which is not likely to be a problem in a survival situation) and by limiting activity in order to decrease energy expended, the metabolic rate is greatly reduced, which in turn reduces wastes and cuts down on the amount of water required by the kidneys. Minimal energy expenditure also reduces the amount of perspiration needed to cool the body, and since you are breathing slowly instead of panting from over-exertion the loss of water through the lungs is dramatically reduced. So take it easy! Conserve your energy, and evaluate all movements of activity carefully beforehand to insure that they are absolutely necessary and that the maximum efficiency is obtained from them. **Ration your sweat, but not your water.**

In hot weather, **keep your shirt on.** Clothing retards perspiration evaporation by holding it on your body in order to get the maximum cooling effect. Light clothing reflects heat. **Keep in the shade.** Sit on something a few inches off the hot ground. If possible, don't lie on the ground because it may be 30 to 45 degrees cooler one foot above the earth and the difference can save a lot of sweat. If you have to move around to check snares and to construct solar stills, do it at night or early in the morning.

Many plants, such as lupine, collect droplets during the night and a considerable amount of water can be collected early in the morning by placing a piece of plastic on the ground and gently shaking this water onto it, or by sponging it up with a piece of cloth. Two solar stills in a good location will provide all the water that you will need if you practice conserving your sweat.

On the seashore you can usually obtain fresh water by digging a well in the sand above the high tide level. Fresh water is lighter than salt water and tends to float. Dirty or muddy water can be cleared by allowing it to settle for a day. All water should be purified by boiling for five minutes or by using water purification tablets.

In the winter, **when there is snow on the ground, the dangers of dehydration are just as great** as they are in the summer on the desert, and since the body may be using lots of energy to keep warm, the kidneys are working overtime. Drink two or three quarts of water a day.

Your sources of water will depend on the environment. In the desert your best friend will be the solar still. In temperate areas, streams, rivers, ponds, lakes, sloughs and snow will all provide usable water. In the arctic water is available nearly everywhere in the summertime. In the winter melted snow and ice provide it. Sea ice can be used for fresh water if it is old (bluish in color with rounded corners).

In the tropics finding water is usually not a problem, but it should always be purified. Hanging jungle vines, cut off at an angle and then notched a few feet higher up, will provide a cool refreshing water supply.

Solar Still Construction (27.1)

1. **Selecting the site** — it should have a minimum of shade and be located in a low area.
2. **Digging the hole** — it should be bowl-shaped, and about three and one-half feet in diameter and two feet deep. Dig a depression in the bottom of the hole for a water container. Slightly mound the dirt up around the rim of the hole so that it is higher at the rim than the surrounding ground level.
3. **Improving the water yield** — slices of cactus are best, but any greenery will help. Cut and place around the sides of the hole with the cut side out.
4. **Positioning the container and sucking tube** — place container or use aluminum foil to form a container, in the center of the hole bottom with the tubing, (i.e. surgical tubing), strung from the bottom of the container and out over the edge of the hole. The tube can be secured to the edge of the water container with a piece of adhesive tape.
5. **Positioning the plastic** — place the plastic over the hole and with a smooth rock set in the center, adjust it so that it is forming a cone shape with the cone tip directly over the center of the water collector. The rock should be heavy enough to pull the plastic taut. Position plastic evenly around the hole and seal down with dirt.
6. **Precaution** — if polluted water is to be used, dig a trench in the sidewall of the solar still hole and line this trench with a piece of plastic. The polluted water is then placed in this plastic lined trench and is subsequently purified as the water

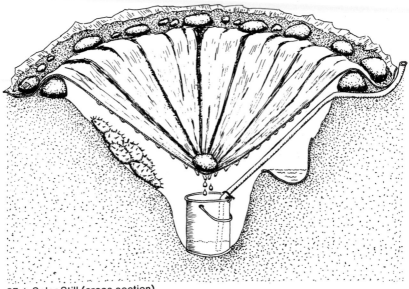

27.1 Solar Still (cross section)

evaporates and condenses on the still cover underside. Avoid splashing polluted water in the container or on the plastic sheet or the rim of the hole contacted by the plastic sheet. The plastic should not touch the inside of the hole or the edge of the container. Remove the plastic as few times as possible for it takes ½ hour or more for the air to become resaturated and the production of water to begin again.

The heat of the sun passes through the plastic and is absorbed by the soil, resulting in the evaporation of the moisture in the earth. This water vapor then condenses on the cooler plastic and the droplets thus formed run down the underside into the waiting container. By the process of capillary action, more water is drawn up to the surface of the soil to replace that which evaporated, and in a good location the still will continue to operate. At night, the rate will be approximately half that of the daytime production. If the supply diminishes after a day or two, it is a simple matter to move the still to a new location. Desert areas, dry washes and depressions are good locations.

Depending on the condition of the soil, the amount of water you can expect to extract in a 24 hour period will vary from one-half pint to three pints. If fresh pieces of vegetation are cut and placed in the hole, this rate can be increased up to two and one-half times the best yield from the soil alone. The still can be used to purify polluted water, urine, sea water, or radiator water (if not contaminated by antifreeze).

The rim of the hole should be raised, as shown in the illustration, so that if it rains, the water which collects in the top of the still will not be contaminated by dirt washing in from along the rim.

A length of surgical tubing (mentioned in Step 4, Solar Still Construction) will enable the distilled water to be drawn directly into the mouth without removing the plastic and without danger of spillage (27.1).

FOOD

Just because you didn't get it at Safeway doesn't mean that it's not edible. **The survivalist must learn to overcome his food prejudices.** Foods that may not look or sound good to eat are often found in the exotic delicacy section with a fancy name like escargot (snail) or are the regular diet of natives (i.e., fish eyes).

We have previously discussed that, depending upon your activity, you can go without food for several weeks. This is not to say, however, that your unfed body will not rebel. The stomach will pang with hunger and the body begins to use up its carbohydrate and fat reserves, then the muscle protein and tendons.

The following information should help you and your stomach to stay on good terms during your wilderness encounter.

1. **Plants**
   a. In general, there is more food value in roots and tubers than in greens.
   b. Do not eat mushrooms unless you are already accustomed to identifying and eating them. They provide little nourishment and a mistake can cause an agonizing death.
   c. Avoid all plants having milky sap, unless familiar with the edible exceptions such as dandelions, wild figs, and papaya.
   d. Tea made by simmering the chopped needles from fir, pine, spruce or hemlock trees is good and contains ascorbic acid needed to prevent scurvy. Rose hips, violet leaves, and wild strawberry leaves are excellent sources of vitamin C. The body does not store this vitamin, thus making fresh meat, greens, berries, tea, etc., an extremely important part of the wilderness diet.
   e. Cattail root and young shoots are excellent eating. The pollen is mostly protein and can be used as flour to make crude biscuits which may not taste like mother's, but are nourishing.
   f. The inner bark of many trees is edible and nutritious. Among the trees which bark can be used for food include the poplars (such as the cottonwoods, as-

pens, willows and birches) and the conifers (cone bearing trees). After first removing the outer bark, the inner bark can be stripped or scraped from the trunk and eaten fresh, dried or cooked. It is most palatable when newly formed in the spring, and at this time of the year in mountainous country, it is frequently the only reliable source of plant food.

g. Most blue and blackberries are edible. Red berries are sometimes. Most white berries are poisonous.
h. Avoid plants resembling beans, cucumbers, melons or parsnips. Some are extremely poisonous.
i. Many nuts are edible including beechnut, butternut, chestnut, filbert, hazelnut, hickory, pinon, sweet acorn and walnuts.
j. Avoid eating the nuts or seeds of fruits; some are poisonous.
k. Plants with orange, yellow, red, dark or soapy-tasting sap, or sap which turns black rapidly upon exposure to the air, should be avoided.
l. No plant resembling dill, parsley, parsnips or with carrot-like foliage, should be eaten.
m. Because an animal eats a certain plant does not mean that it is fit for humans. Horses eat poison ivy; squirrels eat all mushrooms; bears eat baneberry; and birds eat plant seeds containing strychnine.
n. All grass seeds are edible. However, avoid grass seeds which have turned black.

2. Amphibians:
Frogs and salamanders are edible. Remove the skin before cooking. Some species secrete irritating and poisonous fluids from their skins. The salamander tail and frog legs are the most desirable parts; however, the entire body can be consumed. It may be boiled or roasted.

3. Birds:
All birds are edible. Their unspoiled eggs are also edible, even though there is a live embryo inside. Pick (pluck) birds instead of skinning them. More of the fatty tissue is in the skin.

4. **Fish:**
   a. Fish found in North American waters are edible.
   b. Fish heads of small fish make an excellent soup, so don't discard them. Meat in the head (cheek) of some larger fish (i.e., salmon and trout) is excellent eating.
   c. After cleaning and cooking small fish, eat both meat and bones. The small, soft bones of these fish offer a source of calcium.
   d. To obtain the greatest food value from fish, boil or bake them in a rock oven. After boiling fish, drink the remaining water, as the nutrition that was lost from the fish in cooking remains in the water.
   e. Fish may be preserved for relatively long periods by smoking. This process involves the intense smoke exposure of cleaned and dried meat to the fire smoke of deciduous (leaf bearing) trees, preferably apple wood, aspen, hickory and the like. The time required depends upon the size of the fish being smoked, but a wrinkled, smoke-brown, jerky appearance indicates doneness.

5. **Insects:**
   a. The larvae or grubs of many insects are edible and very nourishing. Grubs are found in rotten logs, in the ground and under the bark of dead trees. They should be boiled or fried but can be eaten raw. They also make a fine addition to soups.
   b. Grasshoppers should have the wings, legs, and head removed before cooking as some contain harmful parasites. The body can then be baked between leaves in the coals of a fire, or baked unprotected on hot flat rocks.
   c. Ants are also edible; however, they are more trouble than the food value justifies.

6. **Reptiles:**
   Snakes and lizards are good to eat. Cut the heads off, remove the entrails, pull skin off in banana fashion, and they are ready for the pot.

7. **Rodents:**
   a. Small rodents such as mice can be skinned, feet removed, eviscerated (en-

trails removed), and pounded until all the bones are ground, head included, and used for stew meat.

b. Larger rodents such as squirrels and rabbits are skinned.

Skinning procedure:
(1) Cut around each leg at first joint above foot.
(2) Cut skin on the two rear legs from the first cut to the base of the tail.
(3) Lift and pull skin from each leg, working toward the tail.
(4) Continue pulling toward rib cage and front legs.
(5) Pull front legs out of skin and continue pulling until the skin is over the head and ears.

Dressing procedure:
(1) Cut from anal vent to the throat, being careful to girdle the genitals and anus, which will in step 3, be removed along with the entrails.
(2) The rib cage and pelvic bone can be cut by placing a hunting knife blade under the bone structure and lifting.
(3) The animal can now be eviscerated
(4) Blood residue can be cleaned out by wiping or washing with water.

8. Sea Foods:

a. During summer months, mussels rapidly assimilate certain toxins present in the water and eating them at this time can result in a paralytic poisoning. Avoid eating mussels from April through October. At other times of the year they can be steamed like clams. They are found in large quantities clinging to rocks along the beach at low tide.

b. Avoid eating dead shellfish, or taking shellfish from a bed where you find large quantities of dead ones.

c. Sea urchins look like animated purple or green pincushions and are edible. Break open and eat raw the large red or yellow egg masses.

d. All seaweeds are edible.

e. Snails and limpets creeping on rocks are edible and usually plentiful. Cook by steaming or boiling.

9. Green Algae:

Admittedly not appealing to the eye, but nutritionally speaking, this scummy matter contains more easily digested protein than equal amounts of wheat or potatoes. Edible in either the soupy liquid state or the dried form, algae has a taste roughly comparable to raw pumpkin.

Cooking makes food safer by killing harmful bacteria and parasites. Boiling is the best way to cook food as it preserves all of the juices. Another excellent method is to wrap food in leaves or seaweed and bury in a preheated rock-lined pit from which the fire has been removed. Cover the wrapped food with more leaves and then a layer of dirt. After several hours dig up dinner, strip off the leaves or seaweed and eat.

SNARES AND DEADFALLS

Catching an animal in a snare usually involves placing a loop of wire in such a position that will permit the animal to run into it in the course of its normal activities. The loop should be large enough to admit the head, but not the rest of the body. To assure that the animal enters the loop, use sticks, rocks or brush to direct the path of the animal into the snare (35.1). A small peg with the top split and the bottom of the loop inserted in the crack will hold the loop in position. The bottom of the loop should be about leg high on the animal being snared. The eye in the end of the wire which forms the loop should have at least six twists, and the same for the other end, whether it is attached directly to an anchor or is first attached to a piece of fishline or cord. The latter is a good plan because the line absorbs any twisting instead of the wire (35.1). This is a very effective type of snare and takes little work to set. Set them in runways in the snow or grass or at the entrances to dens or holes in the ground where tracks or fresh digging indicate the presence of animals.

If cord or string is used for a snare loop, it will need to be held in position by small twigs or twisted pieces of grass. However, placement of these items must not hinder or prevent the noose from closing easily on the animal's neck.

Don't move the snare if it falls to yield results in the first day; frequently the second or third day will produce. Also, the less you disturb the area in which a snare is set, the more likely it will be effective.

A lifting branch or pole (37.1) used with the snare will lift the snared animal out of the reach of predators and will also help to prevent twisting and possible breakage of the wire. If no lifting pole is convenient, or if it is cold enough to freeze in a bent position, then use a weight suspended over a limb so that when the snare is tripped the falling weight will lift the animal the desired distance off the ground.

Heavier snares can be made by doubling and twisting the wire together to form a reinforced loop. Some animals can succeed in chewing through a snare, so for some small game animals this procedure is well worth the time. Adjust the size and type of

35.1 Small Animal Snare

snare or deadfall to the animal you wish to catch. It is pointless to set a trap or snare just anywhere. Set it where the game lives, feeds or travels.

Snare loops for rabbits should be about four inches above the ground, with the loop itself set four inches in diameter. Squirrels and chipmunks can be caught by placing a series of wire snares along active trailways (36.1). **Animals, like humans, follow the path of least resistance.** Frequently you will see squirrels running along logs or branches rather than through the brush or vegetation.

Another method that is useful for catching small game is the deadfall set with a "figure 4" trigger (36.2). This can be set in runways, or it can be baited. The part which falls on the animal should be heavy enough to kill it. Flat rocks make good deadfalls. If a limb or log is used, guide stakes driven in the ground on either side of the raised end will insure that it falls directly on the animal.

Shore birds and some ducks can be caught on a fish hook if it is baited and left tied on the beach with a short length of string.

All snares and deadfalls should be kept simple and should be put in place before dark. Use the entrails of previously caught animals for bait. Any place used as a butchering or cleaning area will attract other animals.

36.1 Series Snare

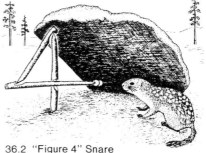
36.2 "Figure 4" Snare

37.1 Spring Snare

FISHING

Fish hooks and lines are the essential items, and since they are difficult to improvise from native materials, take care of them and keep the hooks sharp. Tie two or three feet of leader material to the fish line and attach the hook to the end of the leader using the clinch knot (39.2). A willow or other green branch makes an improvised pole. It is a good idea to place guides along the pole rather than to tie the line directly to the end of the pole. These guides can be made using a bent safety pin (39.1) or snare wire (by twisting a small loop in the wire and affixing it to the pole). Thread the fishing line through the guides and tie it securely to the base of the pole. This permits better casting and playing of the fish, and should a large fish break the tip off the pole, you still have the gear and maybe the fish.

Use natural bait, such as grasshoppers, worms and grubs, when available. Artificial lures can be made from pieces of brightly colored cloth, feathers or foil. Several short, baited lines hanging in the water from branches or tied to floats will frequently catch fish during the night or when you are otherwise occupied.

A primitive, yet strong, fishing line can be created by stripping the cambium layer (a silky, stringy, fibrous tissue within the plant stalk) of the Stinging Nettle (Urtica dioica). Instructions for making fishing line and heavier cordage is found on page 51.

Although this does produce excellent cordage, it is a far simpler task to include a length of fly line as recommended in the Survival Gear Appendix.

In fresh water the best place to fish is in the deeper water. In shallow streams fish the pools below falls, foot of rapids or behind rocks. When fishing from a river bar cast your line to the side where the current flows away from the bar. It is normally in this area where the fish feed on the food particles carried by the current over and around the bar. The most ideal time to fish is in the early morning or early to late evening, although moonlight fishing can be done if you have a light to attract the fish.

Unless you are successful at catching quite a few fish, don't spend too much time and energy trying. It may be more profitable to pick berries or to set additional snares.

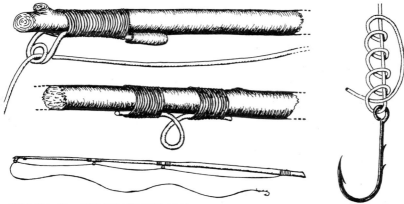

39.1 Primitive Fish Pole Construction

39.2 Clinch Knot

Key can opener

Piece of wood or bone

Safety pin

TRAVEL

As a general rule there is a **higher probability of rescue if the survivalist stays put** and concentrates his efforts, after securing the immediate needs, on making himself easily located. Application of this rule has many advantages, particularly when a downed aircraft or disabled vehicle is involved. In these instances the unit is more easily spotted when it is the object of an aerial search. Parts of the aircraft or vehicle body can provide shelter, fuel and other equipment for survival. By staying you will avoid the hazards, hardships and the waste of precious energy involved in travel.

Perhaps the best advice to give the wilderness traveler or potential wilderness traveler (i.e., a pilot) is to **file a hike, travel or flight plan.** Let someone know where you intend to go and how long you expect to be. This accomplishes two important things. The first is obvious: someone knows approximately where and for how long. The second is as important, but not so obvious: the psychological value of knowing, as a survivalist, that you will become the object of a search.

Rules do have exceptions, however. So if circumstances, after considering your physical condition, the weather, distances, terrain, and your food, water and fuel supplies, dictate that you must travel, keep the following points in mind:

1. Leave a note which can be easily seen that states the date, time and direction you intend to take. A large arrow made of rocks or pieces of bark will do the job.

2. Plan an objective or destination; plot your course and stick to it.

3. If you follow a stream, it is usually easier to **walk along one of the adjacent slopes,** keeping an eye on the stream, than to follow the stream bank which will often be very bushy and brushy. If you are high enough to see out, you are at a better advantage for signaling and for checking landmarks to keep on a definite course.

4. Leave a trail. Break off twigs, leave tracks and notes in muddy places, blaze trees and leave scraps of clothing.

5. Make camp early in the afternoon to allow ample time to build a shelter and fire. Begin your travel early in the morning.

6. Desert travel should not be considered unless you are certain that you can reach your destination on your available water supply. Distances on the desert are most deceiving. A distant rock formation or mountain may be many miles farther than it appears. Travel at night if possible and seek shade and rest during the day.

7. It is usually **colder down in a canyon** or creek bottom than on a hillside above.

8. A slow steady pace is best. Take your time. Short rest periods of about five minutes each hour are advisable.

9. In crossing rivers or streams on foot, **use a stout stick** for extra support and to probe for sudden drop-offs or holes.

10. It is unwise to take chances by jumping over obstacles or sliding down inclines. A sprained ankle or broken bone is most inconvenient.

11. Traveling in deep snow is very difficult without skis or snowshoes. You will get wet from snow and perspiration, and the energy expenditures will be tremendous. When exhaustion forces you to stop, your wet clothing will provide little comfort against chill, and with your body reserves depleted, you are a prime candidate to become another "died of exposure" (hypothermia) statistic. If you must travel in deep snow, spend a day constructing a pair of snowshoes. (See page 56.) You will be repaid for your time and energy after traveling 200 yards.

12. In cold weather adjust clothing and limit exercise to **avoid perspiration.** Sweat-soaked clothing loses its insulating properties and can freeze solid when activity ceases.

13. If you have no map, **use the compass** as described to stay on the course which you have decided to take.

COMPASS

If you are traveling cross country, **use the compass and trust it completely.** As indicated in the section on survival equipment, the compass should be degree-marked for 360 degrees and easily read. To get an accurate reading, the compass should be on a flat surface and at least ten feet from all metal objects. The needle on the compass always points to magnetic north. Align the "N" on the degree scale of your compass with the needle. This gives you the heading of the magnetic North Pole.

The direction to which your indicator points is, however, different from the geographical true North Pole. In fact, the magnetic North Pole lies near the Prince of Wales Island in northern Canada, approximately 1,000 miles south of the geographic true north. For this reason, depending upon your location, a variation must be made to arrive at a heading of true north. This variation may be as great as 20 degrees in the contiguous United States. Because maps are made in coordination with true north one must know how to make this variation.

From a point at the magnetic North Pole, passing through the Great Lakes and extending southward along the coast of Florida the two poles are aligned and no variation is required. This imaginary line is known as the agonic line (43.1).

To find true north while west of the agonic line, align the "N" of the compass with the needle. Rotate the compass counterclockwise to reflect the number of degrees indicated by the isogonic line nearest you (43.1). For example, if you are located near Butte, Montana, rotate the compass 18 degrees counterclockwise. Following this adjustment, the needle now points to the 18 degree mark on the compass. The compass "N" is now pointing true north.

To find true north while east of the agonic line, again line up the needle and the "N" marking on the compass. Rotate the compass clockwise the number of degrees indicated. For example, if you are located near Richmond, Virginia, rotate the compass clockwise 7 degrees. The needle now reads 353 degrees. Again the "N" marking is pointing toward true north while the needle is still pointing magnetic north.

On the floating disc type compass the same isogonic adjustments are made.

However, where on the needle compass the needle always points magnetic north, on the floating disc type compass, the "N" on the disc always points magnetic north. The permanent marking on the disc compass face, after the variation has been made, points true north. Consequently, in the example, following the adjustment for the variation at Butte, the permanent marking is on 340 degrees. This heading reflects true north. In the Richmond example, the permanent mark is on 8 degrees, reflecting true north.

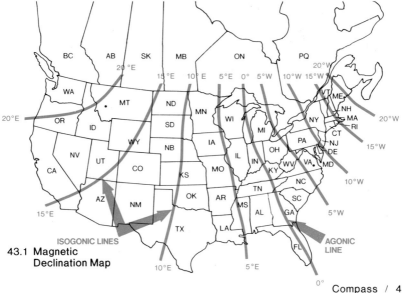

43.1 Magnetic Declination Map

MAP ORIENTATION

Selecting the proper map will aid in the speed and accuracy of your orientation. There are a great many types of maps, and the detail on them will vary. The U.S. Geological Survey maps with a scale of one inch to approximately one mile are recommended. These maps carry a fair amount of detail, including contour lines representing every 80 feet of elevation and geographic coordinates. It is good practice for the backpacker to familiarize himself with this map in advance of a trip.

The first step in map orientation is to align the northern vertical edge so it is facing true north rather than magnetic north. This is accomplished by placing the map on a flat surface and setting the compass upon it. Rotate the map and compass until the compass direction indicator is pointing magnetic north and is in line with the northern vertical edge of the map (45.1). Next follow the procedures in the compass section to correct for true north. Rotate the map with the compass on it to make the true north correction for both the compass and map. The map is now oriented and all mountains, streams, and other landmarks are in their correct relationship relative to your position. Determine the direction you wish to travel noting how this heading compares in relationship to the direction indicator on your compass. This, then, is your heading. **A small scratch or piece of tape** on the compass will insure recall of this heading. Keep in mind that any deviation from this course, due to local terrain, obstacles, etc., will require re-evaluation of map orientation.

Pick a distant tree or other landmark that lies directly in line with this heading. Proceed to the selected landmark, check the compass and continue on the same heading to the next selected point. For example, align the compass with true north. The landmark you have selected is off to your left. Check the approximate degree heading of the landmark in relationship to your compass and see that it is about 40 degrees counterclockwise from north. The heading, then, is 320 degrees. Travel, selecting land marks along this heading.

45.1 Map Orientation

SIGNALING

Perhaps by now, after learning all about survival, and becoming an experienced survivalist, you are finding that you enjoy this new environment. This environment of no time clocks, polluted air, or crowded highways you find has spoiled you, and now you aren't all that anxious to be found. However, if you must get back, a few pointers on signaling techniques are in order.

1. The purpose of a signal is to increase your findability and to provide information about your condition and position (i.e., direction of the smoke drift from your signal fire will tell a pilot from which direction and position to make an air drop).
2. Select the location for each signal carefully and determine what types of signal options you have and which will be the most effective to relay your position and condition.
3. Have signals prepared or available for immediate use.
4. If firewood is scarce, or you have battery powered signaling devices, pyrotechnics (i.e., aerial signal flares), smoke flares, etc., don't use these signals indiscriminately.

The signaling methods listed and described below are those which are the most widely used and most frequently available to the survivalist.

Fire and Smoke Signals:
Age-old signals have been smoke by day, and fire by night. The accepted method for emergency signaling with fire is to lay out three, about 100 feet apart (either in line or triangular). Although this sounds good and does work well under ideal conditions (ample dry fuel, etc.), in practicality, count your blessings if you have one fire and enough fuel to keep it going. During the night the flames should be as bright as possible, and during the day smoke should be produced.

Attempt to create smoke which contrasts with its background. Dark smoke against snow and white smoke against darker ground or background. Here again, as a practical matter, any color smoke will do. Normally, what would be required to get

In constructing the signal, use straight lines and definite angles and place the signal in an area providing maximum visibility from the air.

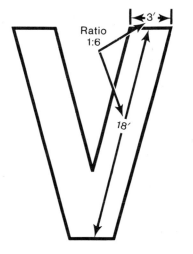

Ratio 1:6

3'

18'

Require Medical Assistance	X
Require Assistance	V
Yes - Affirmative	Y
No - Negative	N
Proceeding in this direction	↑

47.1 Ground Signals & Construction

dark smoke won't be available unless you have a downed aircraft or stalled vehicle because the darkest smoke is the product of oil-soaked rags, pieces of rubber and some plastics. White smoke, on the other hand, can be made by adding green leaves, ferns, damp grass, moss or even a little water to the fire.

Smoke signals are most effective on relatively calm and clear days. Wind, rain and snow tend to disperse the smoke. Also, smoke signaling is unreliable in densely wooded areas. Open terrain is best. If you intend to rely on signal fires and your location and weather suggest an aerial search, the fire must be prepared prior to the time the aircraft enters the area.

Ground and Shadow Signals:
This type of signal is easy to construct and works for you unattended. These signals are mounds constructed of brush, foliage, rocks or snow blocks. These mounds should be constructed in one of the international distress patterns pictured and described in 47.1. The effectiveness of this signal is the shadow cast by it when the sun is present, so the shadow signal needs to be oriented to the sun. In the areas of North America to which this book applies, it is required that an east-west line of signal be constructed. The resulting shadow is to the north of the signal line. The more material used, the more conspicuous the shadow cast. Shadows thus formed are visible for many miles from the air.

In the snow, tramp out trenches to form signal letters. Outline them with pieces of bark or fir branches placed on the snow near the edge of the trench. These give excellent shadow effects and color contrasts.

Mirror Signals: (Instructions) 49.1
1. Reflect sunlight from mirror front onto a nearby surface.
2. Slowly raise mirror to eye-level a few inches from the face and look through the sighting hole.
3. A spot of sunlight coming through the hole will fall upon the face, hand, or shirt and you will see its reflection in the rear face of the mirror. This spot of light is the aim indicator.

49.1 Using the Signal Mirror

4. Now, while sighting the plane through the hole, adjust the angle of the mirror until the reflection of the spot of light in step 3 disappears through the hole. You are now on target.

5. Do not continue to flash the mirror after your signal has been acknowledged because the flash can blind the pilot. Flash it only occasionally to keep him on course.

Practice using the mirror on near objects and keep it on your person at all times. Use the mirror freely. Even on hazy days the flash of the mirror can be seen before the survivalist can see the aircraft. For this reason the mirror can be flashed in the direction of the sound of the aircraft, even though you cannot see it.

Battery-powered Signals:

All battery-powered equipment such as radios, locator beacons and flashlights, are not always 100 percent reliable in an emergency. A battery has a limited amount of energy and deteriorates with age. Cold temperatures reduce battery life and output. If you carry independent battery-operated emergency signaling equipment, remember to check it at frequent intervals (at least every thirty days). If the manufacturer lists an expected battery life or expiration date on the battery, this should be noted on the cover of the device. Don't try to stretch this date. Discard the battery even though it still seems to be operational. In cold weather keep battery-operated equipment next to your body and under your clothing to keep it warm. In warm weather keep the equipment in the shade. The general thought on this type of equipment is that while it is good, and can serve the purpose, don't trust your life to it. There are other ways to attract searchers. **The International Morse Code emergency distress signal is S(...)O(---)S(...).** This can be sent with a flashlight. Use the flash button. The dots should be three in sequence. The dashes should be twice as long as the dots. Use the flashlight at night and when you have some hope of its being seen.

Pyrotechnic signaling equipment is primarily intended for night use, and also should only be used when you hear an aircraft or ground searcher.

The whistle, like the signal mirror, should be carried on your person and ready for immediate use.

CORD AND ROPE MAKING

A primitive, yet strong, fishing line can be created by stripping the cambium layer (a silky, stringy, fibrous tissue within the plant stalk) of the Stinging Nettle (Urtica dioica). The dried stalk of the mature plant yields the most durable strands. After pounding and removing the pulp and wood material, the fibre is easily removed and cleaned by passing it between the fingers. Knot and tie the ends of several strands (for heavier duty cordage) or loop a single strand around a braiding point (anchor) and proceed to simultaneously twist and braid (51.1), introducing new and alternating length strands one and one-half to two inches prior to reaching the end of the previously braided cordage (51.2). These new strands are themselves twisted into the preceding strand ends and the braid is continued.

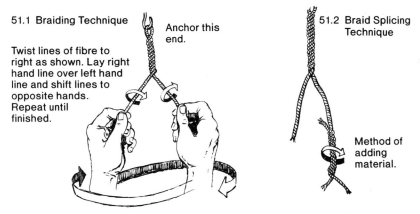

51.1 Braiding Technique

Anchor this end.

Twist lines of fibre to right as shown. Lay right hand line over left hand line and shift lines to opposite hands. Repeat until finished.

51.2 Braid Splicing Technique

Method of adding material.

KNOTS

In the extreme, your life could depend on your ability to select and tie the proper knot. Fortunately, in most instances, a poorly selected or a poorly tied knot is just a nuisance (i.e., the loss of a fish, a poorly constructed snare, or a tarp which blows down in the middle of the night).

The few knots selected and illustrated in this section are the most common and useful ones needed in the wilderness survival situation.

Square Knot (53.1)

This knot is used primarily for joining two ends of a cord together, as in the case of bundling several items about the girth with a single rope. Although this knot is exceptionally strong under tension, it has the serious disadvantage of jamming up tight under great tension.

Sheet Bend (53.2)

The sheet bend is used to join two ropes of different thicknesses together. The larger diameter rope is referred to as the bend. The smaller rope is pushed up through the loop and around the larger rope. This knot is used for temporarily fastening a rope to the bight or bend of another rope or to an eye.

Bowline (53.3)

Use this knot when a nonslipping loop is required but one that can be easily released. The loop formed by this knot can be placed over a rock or sturdy branch to lower oneself; then simply flip-roll the rope and the loop will release off the rock or branch and the rope is available to use again.

Double Half Hitch (53.4)

The single half hitch is the basic initial knot used in the formation of a number of other knots. Although rarely used alone, two consecutive half hitches are an excellent way to secure a rope to a branch or similar object.

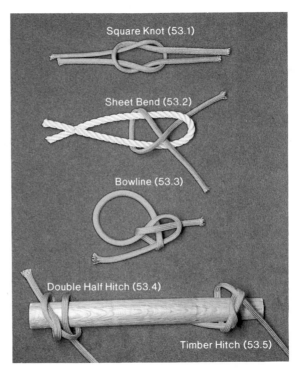

Square Knot (53.1)

Sheet Bend (53.2)

Bowline (53.3)

Double Half Hitch (53.4)

Timber Hitch (53.5)

Timber Hitch (53.5)

This knot is normally used when a rope is to be quickly, but temporarily, tied to a log or piece of timber. The timber hitch does not hold secure unless taut.

It should be noted that the **weakest portion of a rope or cord is at the knot.** For instance, if the simple overhand knot is allowed to remain in a section of rope, the knotted portion possesses less than half the breaking-strength of the unknotted rope.

METEOROLOGY
(Weather and Climate Phenomena)

Some practical information about meterology can influence a number of decisions to be made by the survivalist. The wind direction and velocity, local temperatures, and indications of the weather tomorrow are factors to consider in shelter type and construction, fire building, placing traps and shares, signaling, etc.

Temperature decreases as elevation increases (an average of 3½ degrees F. per 1000 feet, depending on the locality, time of day, and the season). Also, with each 600 miles in latitudinal (angular distance north or south from the earth's equator) change is roughly equal to an elevational change equal to 1000 feet; or again, reflecting a 3½ degree average temperature variation. Of course, variations may be much greater due to a variety of circumstances. For instance, in January the average sea-level temperature may range from 60 degrees F. in southern Texas, 40 degrees in Kansas, 20 degrees in North Dakota and 0 degrees in northern Manitoba.

In rugged terrain gentle to moderate winds are frequently generated as a character of that topography. During the evening and night time a downslope movement of cool air creates a mountain breeze. Conversely, during the day a valley breeze initiates when heated air expands, rising along valley slopes creating the upslope movement of warm air.

Cloud types and conditions are frequently good weather predictors.

Cumulus clouds — broken clouds, generally under 5000 feet — fair weather.

Nimbostratus — solid storm clouds, 4000 to 7000 feet — rain or snow.

Altostratus — high elevation gray sheet clouds, 15,000 feet — rain, snow or wind.

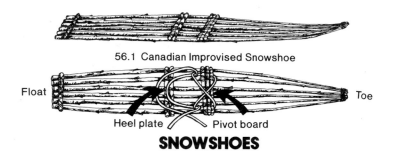

56.1 Canadian Improvised Snowshoe

Float   Toe

Heel plate   Pivot board

SNOWSHOES

The Canadian improvised snowshoe (56.1) has been adopted by the United States Air Force Survival School due to its ease of construction and the minimal number of tools and materials required to make it.

Select six poles (12 for two shoes) 6′ in length (or individual's height), thumb size at base and little finger size at the tip. Cut six (12 for two shoes) sticks roughly 10″ long and ¾″ thick and lash them as follows:

a. Lash one stick to the snowshoe float area. Cut off excess.

b. Lash three sticks forward of the center of the shoe to form the pivot board. This position of pivot board allows the float to remain on the snow and causes the tip to rise when walking.

c. Lash two sticks where your heel strikes the snowshoe to form the heel plate.

d. Tie the snowshoe tips together.

The snowshoe binding (56.1, 56.2) must be secured to the snowshoe so that the survivalist's foot can pivot when walking. Braided nylon cord is best, however even braided flyline (51.1, 51.2) is adequate.

56.2 Snowshoe Harness

The American improvised snowshoe (57.1), although more difficult to construct, has the advantage of being lighter. Cut two pieces (4 for two shoes) of green wood about 5′ in length, large thumb size at the base tapering to the tip, and two sticks (4 for two shoes) 8-9″ long and ¾″ thick.

a. Notch and bevel ends of 5′ sticks and cut rectangular notches for crosspieces (1¼″ x ⅜″ deep). Shape crosspieces to fit as shown (57.1).

b. Lash double length of cord around side pieces 4-5 inches behind the forward crosspiece, twisting it tight with two sticks about 6″ by ½″ thick. Allow a 5-6″ opening between them for toe room. Secure the ends to crosspieces. Lash toe and heel ends.

c. Lace with rawhide, cord, etc., using a half hitch pattern with heavier material in the center for foot support. Short sticks can be used to twist webbing tight.

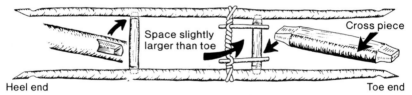

Space slightly larger than toe

Cross piece

Heel end

Toe end

57.1 American Improvised Snowshoe

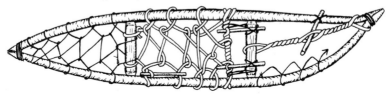

EDIBLE PLANTS

PLANTS AS FOOD

As the harvesting of wild plants becomes increasingly popular we are compelled to make a few important comments concerning this practice.

First, although the plants selected for these manuals are generally widespread, numerous, and probably not in jeopardy of becoming an endangered plant species (the single exception is *Brodiaea pulchella,* the Wild Hyacinth), there are those species which qualify as being rare and, consequently, should only be harvested in an emergency. This is particularly true of some of the higher elevation plants such as the Avalanche Lily (*lilium* species). As a general rule we recommend that there be at least ten of a species present in an area before considering harvest of a single plant.

Secondly, not all plants of the same species necessarily taste the same. There are other factors which govern the taste character of identical plant species in different locations apart from degree of plant maturity. Soil conditions and amount of moisture are two important variables which may control whether one of a species is somewhat bitter and another bland.

Thirdly, the nutritional value of native wild plants is adequately demonstrated by the foraging mammals and birds, Indians, and early settlers. Carbohydrates, proteins, vitamins, and even minerals are found in nearly all plants (particularly the plant seeds). While most wild plants are no longer used as dietary staples by humans except in an emergency, it does not alter the fact that wild plants can supply nearly every nutritional need known.

Lastly, an unidentified plant should be considered poisonous. Some wild plants are moderately to extremely poisonous to humans (see **About Poisonous Plants,** pg. 226). Many an early settler and his 20th Century counterpart have died eating Poison Hemlock *(Conium maculatum),* Destroying Angel *(Amanita verna),* and Death Camas *(Zigadenus paniculatus),* each of which has a reasonable look-alike edible plant. Also, it should be mentioned that there is no such thing as a safe, general edibility test. In the case of some plants, such as Poison Hemlock and Destroying Angel, they should never enter the mouth under any circumstances.

ABOUT PLANT NAMES

In order to provide means for naming plants by which all peoples, regardless of language or nationality, could relate, Latin was selected as the international language of botanists. The scientific name, then, is formulated in accordance with the principles of Latin grammar to create a uniformity within the worldwide botanical community for name and identification of each plant type or kind.

What has subsequently evolved is a system of plant classification in accordance with their presumed natural relationships. This science is called *taxonomy*. Put another way, plant taxonomy is the science of collecting, describing, naming, and classifying plants.

Plant taxonomy, by its very nature, is not a totally exact science, and there is occasionally some disagreement among taxonomic botanists. This lack of agreement normally involves the number of species within a genus. Less frequently it involves which species should be included in a particular genus. But, by-and-large, agreement does exist, and for our purposes this does not pose a significant problem.

The present categories of classification in the plant kingdom are:

1. Divisions
2. Subdivisions
3. Classes
4. Subclasses
5. Orders
6. Suborders
7. Families
8. Subfamilies (also called tribes)
9. Genera
10. Subgenera (also called sections)
11. Species
12. Subspecies
13. Varieties
14. Forms

Normally it is not necessary to go through this complete classification list when referring to a particular plant. The *genus* (the category or main subdivision within a specific plant family) and *species* (related plants under the main subdivision) are generally all that is needed in identifying a plant. Use this method for identification along with a common plant name.

① SUNFLOWER

② *Helianthus annuus* ③ COMPOSITAE ④ Sunflower family

⑤ **Other Common Names:** Common Sunflower, *H. annuus:* Kansas Sunflower

⑥ **Description:** *Helianthus:* Coarse annual or perennial herb 3 dm to 3 m tall; leaves simple, opposite, rough, toothed; large, conspicuous, yellow, ray-like flowers surround red-purple or brown disk-shaped flowers; produces numerous seeds. *.H. annuus:* Erect, stout stemmed, annual herb, 3-20 dm tall; stalk fibrous and prickly hairy; leaves triangular to diamond-egg-shaped; flower up to 15 cm diameter; seed head purplish brown. Drawing is of *H. pumilus,* a perennial.

⑦ **Range:** *Helianthus:* Widely distributed throughout North America; plains, open fields, open woods, and grassy slopes.

⑧ **Season:** Blossoms in April or May, lasts into fall; seeds mature in fall.

⑨ **Edible:** Seeds, roots of some species.

⑩ **Preparation:** Seed head is cut off and seed rubbed or ground out. Seeds parched and eaten, hull and all, or hulled and ground. Hulled seeds are heated (not cooked) for mush. Dark-roasted seed shells can be ground and brewed as coffee. Roots (of edible species, i.e., *H. maximiliannii, H. nuttallii)* are roasted or boiled.

⑪ **Notes of Interest:** Sunflower seeds contain extraordinary nourishment. 100 grams of seed contains 360 calories; seeds are 52% crude protein and 27% carbohydrate.

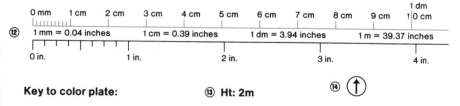

⑫
| 0 mm | 1 cm | 2 cm | 3 cm | 4 cm | 5 cm | 6 cm | 7 cm | 8 cm | 9 cm | 1 dm 10 cm |

1 mm = 0.04 inches   1 cm = 0.39 inches   1 dm = 3.94 inches   1 m = 39.37 inches

0 in.   1 in.   2 in.   3 in.   4 in.

Key to color plate: ⑬ **Ht: 2m**   ⑭ ↑

EXPLANATORY NOTES

Edible Plant

(1) Widely accepted common plant name.

(2) Botanical (scientific) plant name. The first name (i.e., *Helianthus*) is that of the plant genus (the main subdivision within a particular plant family). The second name (i.e., *annuus*) is the plant's specific name.

(3) The scientific family name.

(4) The common family name.

(5) Synonym(s) or nickname(s) by which the plant is known.

(6) Distinguishing characteristics and detailed description of the plant in the color plate.

(7) Indicates the broad range and habitat appearance of the genus (occasionally refers to the specific plant in the color plate).

(8) Refers to the blooming period and/or the edible part availability period. This information frequently applies to other species within the genus as well.

(9) Notes the edible plant part(s).

(10) Describes the manner in which the edible plant part(s) is prepared for eating or drinking.

(11) Interesting miscellaneous information concerning the plant. Frequently the vitamin content and/or food value are herein mentioned.

(12) An equivalency scale for easy translation of the metric measures given in the plant description to the customary (inch) scale.

(13) Refers to the height of the plant in the color plate.

(14) Indicates the top of the color plate.

AMARANTH

Amaranthus retroflexus / **AMARANTHACEAE**   **Amaranth family**

Other Common Names: Green Amaranth, Redroot Pigweed

Description: *Amaranthus:* Coarse, annual herb to 1.5 m tall; stalk tip bears inconspicuous small, green or purple, petalless flowers in dense, scaly clusters; leaves alternate; fruit inflated; shiny black seed. *A. retroflexus:* Erect, coarse, stout stemmed, branching plant, 3-10 dm high; stem and root are red; leaves 7-19 cm long, pale green, broad based, wavy edged and prominently veined on underside.

Range: *Amaranthus:* Found throughout North America below 2500 m in widely varying habitats; often weedy.

Season: Provides edibles in all seasons; most abundant in spring and summer.

Edible: Leaves and shoots before plant blooms; seeds in fall and winter.

Preparation: Leaves and shoots can be eaten raw in the spring and are great for a salad base. As plant matures, steaming or stewing may be preferred. The seeds ripen in fall and can be stripped off, winnowed and parched for an hour before grinding for flour or boiled for mush.

Notes of Interest: The greens are bland to the taste, but are an excellent source of vitamins A and C. There are 30 or more species found in North America.

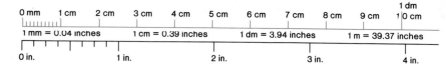

| 0 mm | 1 cm | 2 cm | 3 cm | 4 cm | 5 cm | 6 cm | 7 cm | 8 cm | 9 cm | 1 dm 10 cm |

1 mm = 0.04 inches   1 cm = 0.39 inches   1 dm = 3.94 inches   1 m = 39.37 inches

| 0 in. | 1 in. | 2 in. | 3 in. | 4 in. |

AMERICAN BISTORT

Polygonum bistortoides / **POLYGONACEAE** **Buckwheat family**

Other Common Names: Knotweed, Smartweed, *P. bistortoides:* Mountain Meadow Knotweed

Description: *Polygonum:* Occasionally woody, annual or perennial herbs 1 dm to 4 m tall; jointed stalks sometimes swollen at joint; tissue-like sheaths on stem; leaves alternate, frequently narrow; small flowers red, green or white. *P. bistortoides:* Perennial herb 2-6 dm tall; stems single to multiple; basal leaves long stalked, oblong, 1-4 cm wide, sharply pointed ends, smooth above and minutely hairy below; stem leaves smaller with sheath equaling or exceeding blade length; dense oblong flower cluster 2-4 cm long is white.

Range: *Polygonum:* Widely distributed throughout North America; wide ranging altitudes to alpine summits; mostly in wet places.

Season: Spring through summer; largely dependent upon elevation, with higher elevational plants appearing later.

Edible: Rootstalk, shoots before leaves unfurl.

Preparation: Starchy, fleshy rootstalk is either eaten raw, boiled or roasted. Roasting is superior, preserving the almond flavor. Young shoots are boiled in salted water.

Notes of Interest: The name Bistort is derived from the Latin (bis = twice, torta = twisted) and refers to the twice-twisted character of the rootstalk.

0 mm	1 cm	2 cm	3 cm	4 cm	5 cm	6 cm	7 cm	8 cm	9 cm	1 dm 10 cm

1 mm = 0.04 inches	1 cm = 0.39 inches	1 dm = 3.94 inches	1 m = 39.37 inches

0 in.	1 in.	2 in.	3 in.	4 in.

BALSAMROOT

Balsamorhiza deltoidea / **COMPOSITAE** **Sunflower family**

Other Common Names: Spring Sunflower, Northwest Balsamroot (also spelled Balsam Root)

Description: *Balsamorhiza:* Coarse, low perennial herb to 8 dm tall; large thick woody root supports an erect, mostly naked stem; basal leaves large, elongated, triangular to heart-shaped to .5 dm long with wavy smooth or toothed edges; stem-leaves are oval to lance-like; yellow flower head similar to small sunflower. *B. deltoidea:* Coarse, somewhat hairy basal leaves 1-2.5 dm long, ruffly elongated heart-shaped, rounded lobes, entire or toothed, gradually narrowed at base, conspicuous glands; flowering stems 1 or more, 3-7 dm high, with 1-4 narrow stem leaves.

Range: *Balsamorhiza:* Found in fairly open dry hills and slopes, frequently in stony ground throughout western North America to 2500 m.

Season: Flowers in late April through June. Provides edibles in all seasons.

Edible: The root is edible any time of year, stems and leaves in the spring. After the plant flowers, the seeds may be harvested.

Preparation: The root is best roasted or baked, but is good sliced and sauteed. In early spring the tender young stems and leaves may be eaten raw, used in salads or boiled. The seeds are good raw, or roasted and ground for mush or flour.

Notes of Interest: The dozen or so species of *Balsamorhiza* were important in the diet of Indians of the West.

									1 dm
0 mm	1 cm	2 cm	3 cm	4 cm	5 cm	6 cm	7 cm	8 cm	9 cm	1 0 cm

1 mm = 0.04 inches	1 cm = 0.39 inches	1 dm = 3.94 inches	1 m = 39.37 inches

0 in.	1 in.	2 in.	3 in.	4 in.

Edible Plant

Ht: 6 dm

BISCUITROOT

Lomatium cous / **UMBELLIFERAE** **Parsley family**

Other Common Names: Also Biscuit-root, Desert Parsley

Description: *Lomatium:* Short to absent-stemmed perennials to 6 dm tall; tuber-like to slender root or fleshy corm; leaves mostly basal, compound, variable, irregularly divided; flower head, compound, usually at the end of a leafless, short stem; flowers are yellow, white, pink or purplish. *L. cous:* Scaly minutely haired; stemless, arising from a large, nearly spherical tuber 5-9 cm long; leaves compound feather-like with leaflets divided oblong to lance-like 3-6 mm long; leafless flower stalk 5-15 cm terminates in a 6-12 rayed flower head; many yellow orbicular flowers in each flower head; fruit slenderly oval 5-9 mm.

Range: *Lomatium:* Found in dry ground in the more arid regions of the West. Some species to 3000 m.

Season: Flowers in April and May. Provides edibles mostly in spring and early summer.

Edible: Tubers, flower stems in spring; leaves, flowers and seeds, spring and summer.

Preparation: The tubers of all species are edible. They can be eaten raw or boiled but are best after the plant has flowered; the taste is similar to that of celery. They can be peeled and sun dried or baked and ground into flour. Tea can be made using leaves and flowers. The flower stems and leaves are best in the spring and provide fine greens for a salad.

Notes of Interest: *Lomatium* was a chief article of trade among the Indians.

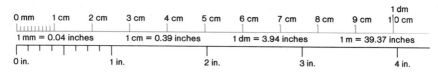

Edible Plant

Ht: 4 dm

BLACKBERRY

Rubus procerus / **ROSACEAE**   **Rose family**

Other Common Names: *R. procerus:* Himalaya Blackberry

Description: *Rubus:* Shrub or bush-like perennial, trailing or climbing, thorned or smooth; leaves simple and lobed to compound; fruit, a berry, generally in multiple drupelets. *R. procerus:* Bushy, large, dense clusters; stems stout, multiple, arching, thorned, up to 10 m long; leaves divided into 3 or 5 leaflets, sharply toothed, 1.5-3.5 cm; fruit, black when mature.

Range: *Rubus:* Found throughout North America, generally in uncultivated and burn areas. Their habitat is extremely varied.

Season: Blooms in spring and early summer; fruit late summer and autumn.

Edible: Young shoots in spring; berries ripen in late summer and autumn.

Preparation: The young shoots can be cut just above the ground, peeled and eaten raw or cooked. Beginning in late summer the berries of most species are available. The berry can be eaten raw, boiled down to a syrup, squeezed for juice, cooked with stews or made into preserves, pies, and even wine. Leaves can be dried and used to make a tea substitute.

Notes of Interest: Noted for its sweet delicious taste. The berries and root have medicinal properties useful for treating diarrhea.

| 0 mm | 1 cm | 2 cm | 3 cm | 4 cm | 5 cm | 6 cm | 7 cm | 8 cm | 9 cm | 1 dm 10 cm |

1 mm = 0.04 inches   1 cm = 0.39 inches   1 dm = 3.94 inches   1 m = 39.37 inches

| 0 in. | 1 in. | 2 in. | 3 in. | 4 in. |

 **Edible Plant**

Ht: 15 dm

BLACKCAP

Rubus leucodermis / **ROSACEAE**   **Rose family**

Other Common Names: Western Blackcap, Wild Raspberry

Description: *Rubus:* Shrub or bush-like perennial, trailing or
climbing, thorned or smooth; leaves simple and lobed to
compound; fruit, a berry, generally in multiple drupelets.
R. leucodermis: Stems densely clustered, 1-2.5 m high,
powdery coated, mature stems bluish; leaves compound
with 3-7 egg-shaped, sharply toothed leaflets with white-
hairy underside; flowers are white; fruit 8-12 mm wide,
grayish in color, covered with fine, short hairs.

Range: *Rubus:* Found throughout North America, generally in uncultivated and burn areas.
Their habitat is extremely varied, depending on the species. *R. leucodermis:* Open woods
from California to British Columbia and east to Wyoming.

Season: Blooms in spring and early summer; fruit late in summer and autumn.

Edible: Young shoots in spring; berries ripen in late summer and autumn.

Preparation: The young shoots can be cut just above the ground, peeled and eaten raw or
cooked. The berry can be eaten raw, boiled down to a syrup, squeezed for juice, cooked
with stews or made into preserves, pies and even wine. Leaves can be dried and used to
make a tea substitute.

Notes of Interest: An astringent, which curbs loss of fluid from the gastrointestinal tract, is
prepared from both the unripe berries and roots. All *Rubus* are high in vitamin C.

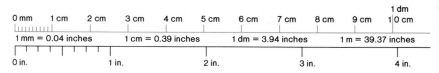

Edible Plant

Ht: 11 dm

BRACKEN FERN

Pteridium aquilinum / **POLYPODIACEAE   Fern family**

Other Common Names: Western Brake-fern, Eagle Fern, Pasture-brake, Fiddlehead (in early stage)

Description: Large, coarse, triangular shaped, light green fronds (leaflike organ of a fern) are 3-forked and up to 1 m in length; mature plant stalk is straw-colored and polished; spreads from creeping root-stalks; hair shoots uncurl in spring resembling fiddleheads; mature plant can exceed 1.5 m tall; mature spores on the frond undersurface have a velvety brown appearance.

Range: Common west of the Rocky Mountains, less so east; found in medium to low altitudes in fields, burns, moist coniferous forests, and rocky canyons.

Season: Appears in early spring as fiddlehead shaped shoots.

Edible: Young shoots in spring, roots in autumn.

Preparation: Snap off young shoots about 15 cm from the curled fiddlehead, discarding the head itself. Peel the remaining shoot and eat raw, cooked (boiled in salted water), or steamed. Autumn rootstalks are edible after removing outer covering and roasting.

Notes of Interest: Historically this plant has been accepted and harvested as a suitable edible. However, new evidence indicates that eating sufficient quantities of this plant over a protracted period may be dangerous to health (see Poisonous Plant Section, page 242).

0 mm	1 cm	2 cm	3 cm	4 cm	5 cm	6 cm	7 cm	8 cm	9 cm	1 dm 1|0 cm
1 mm = 0.04 inches			1 cm = 0.39 inches			1 dm = 3.94 inches			1 m = 39.37 inches	
0 in.			1 in.			2 in.		3 in.		4 in.

Edible Plant

BULRUSH

Scirpus acutus / **CYPERACEAE**   **Sedge family**

Other Common Names: Tule

Description: *Scirpus:* Annual or perennial, small to large grass-like plant 6 cm to 5 m high; pithy stem triangular to circular in cross-section; leaves grass-like or sheath-like; flowers clustered or arranged cylindrically. *S. acutus:* Slender, dark green, 1-3 m high; thick and scaly rootstalks; small basal leaf or sheath; flowers brown.

Range: *Scirpus:* Throughout much of North America in dense stands in shallow water around edges of reservoirs, marshes and swamplands.

Season: Provides edibles throughout the year.

Edible: Young shoots in spring and fall; seeds in fall; rootstalk throughout the year.

Preparation: Harvest young shoots by following the rootstalk which bears the shoots. Shoots should be peeled and eaten raw or cooked. Rootstalk pith (core) is excellent baked. The rootstalk and stem can be dried and pounded into flour and mixed with the seeds for baking. In fall the seeds can be ground into meal.

Notes of Interest: While the mature stems are too tough to be eaten, they can be used for weaving materials — mats, containers, cordage, etc.

0 mm	1 cm	2 cm	3 cm	4 cm	5 cm	6 cm	7 cm	8 cm	9 cm	1 dm 10 cm

1 mm = 0.04 inches   1 cm = 0.39 inches   1 dm = 3.94 inches   1 m = 39.37 inches

0 in.   1 in.   2 in.   3 in.   4 in.

Edible Plant

Ht: 13 dm

BUR REED

Sparganium simplex / **SPARGANIACEAE** **Bur reed family**

Other Common Names: None

Description: *Sparganium:* Aquatic or marsh perennial 1 dm to 2.5 m tall; creeping rootstalk; stems simple or branched; leaves in 2 rows, long, linear, sheathing at base; flowers tiny, compact in spherical head; nut-like fruit. *S. simplex:* Stem erect up to 12 dm high; leaves mostly longer, flat, somewhat ridged; 2-6 flower clusters; fruited heads 15-18 mm diameter.

Range: *Sparganium:* Widely distributed throughout North America; swamps, ponds, shallow water and mud.

Season: Flowers in July and August followed by seed heads; provides edibles nearly year-round.

Edible: Tubers on rootstalk and bulb-like base.

Preparation: Tubers and bulb-like base are edible when cooked (either boiled or roasted). Both tubers and bulb-like base can be dried and pounded into flour.

Notes of Interest: There are both resemblance and habitat similarities between some species of this plant and Cattail *(T. latifolia).* The Cattail, however, has the cylindrical seed head, whereas the Bur reed seed is round and burred, and usually grows on the side of the stalk.

0 mm	1 cm	2 cm	3 cm	4 cm	5 cm	6 cm	7 cm	8 cm	9 cm	1 dm 10 cm

1 mm = 0.04 inches   1 cm = 0.39 inches   1 dm = 3.94 inches   1 m = 39.37 inches

0 in.   1 in.   2 in.   3 in.   4 in.

CAMAS

Camassia quamash / **LILIACEAE** **Lily family**

Other Common Names: Blue Camas, Wild Hyacinth

Description: *Camassia:* Perennial herb with flower stalk 3-8 dm tall; rises from a cluster of slender, grass-shaped, bright green leaves; flowers blue or white, borne along stem on individual stalks. *C. quamash:* Flowering stem 2-6 dm high; leaves generally shorter; egg-shaped bulb; flowers spoke-like, dark blue.

Range: *Camassia:* Plains and moist meadows of the Pacific Northwest to the Rockies to 2500 m.

Season: Blooming period ranges with elevation from late April into June.

Edible: The bulb is the primary food source.

Preparation: The bulb can be obtained with a digging stick, then roasted, baked, boiled, steamed, dried or eaten raw; although boiling does more to soften the starchy bulbs. The bulbs are more nutritious than potatoes.

Notes of Interest: Much colorful history of the Pacific Northwest involves the Camas. The bulb was a staple of the Nez Perce Indians and the Camas meadows were zealously guarded. White settlers and their livestock encroached, destroying this prized food source. The war which ensued between the Nez Perce and the United States Government was one of the most interesting, yet tragic, wars of intra-American history.

| 0 mm | 1 cm | 2 cm | 3 cm | 4 cm | 5 cm | 6 cm | 7 cm | 8 cm | 9 cm | 1 dm 10 cm |

1 mm = 0.04 inches   1 cm = 0.39 inches   1 dm = 3.94 inches   1 m = 39.37 inches

| 0 in. | 1 in. | 2 in. | 3 in. | 4 in. |

Edible Plant

Ht: 3 dm

CANDY FLOWER

Montia sibirica / **PORTULACACEAE   Purslane family**

Other Common Names: Western Spring Beauty, Siberian Miner's Lettuce

Description: *Montia:* Succulent, small, annual or perennial herb 2 cm to 5 dm high; leaves basal, opposite or alternate; flowers borne along stem or in umbrella-like array. *M. sibirica:* Annual herb 1-5 dm high; stems few to many; basal leaves, egg-shaped to broadly diamond-shaped, occasionally lance-like 2-7 cm long; upper stem leaves stalkless, opposing pairs; loosely flowered, one to several per stem, pink in color.

Range: *Montia:* Primarily in western North America in moist woods in partial shade to 2200 m.

Season: Blossoms in early spring and flowers frequently last to late summer; edible from spring to fall.

Edible: Stems, leaves and roots.

Preparation: Leaves and stems are eaten raw. Excellent mixed with Watercress and used as a salad. Although this plant can be used as a potherb, it is much more nutritious raw. Like *M. perfoliata,* it is a gourmet treat when served over Rainbow trout in a root flour bread sandwich.

Notes of Interest: *M. sibirica* was originally discovered in Siberia in 1753. *Montia* and *Claytonia* genus are similar; however the *Montia* genus does not have corms.

0 mm	1 cm	2 cm	3 cm	4 cm	5 cm	6 cm	7 cm	8 cm	9 cm	1 dm 10 cm

1 mm = 0.04 inches	1 cm = 0.39 inches	1 dm = 3.94 inches	1 m = 39.37 inches

0 in.	1 in.	2 in.	3 in.	4 in.

CATTAIL

Typha latifolia / **TYPHACEAE** **Cattail family**

Other Common Names: *T. latifolia:* Broad-leaved Cattail

Description: *Typha:* Marsh perennial with stout stem to 2.5 m tall; leaves, light green, linear, sword shaped and spongy, frequently higher than flower; flowers in dense, cylinder shaped, spike, brown in color. *T. latifolia:* Slightly broader leaf than *T. angustifolia;* single spiked head.

Range: *Typha:* Widely distributed throughout North America; ditches, ponds, swamps, along streams and in marshy areas.

Season: Provides edibles throughout the year.

Edible: Young shoots and flower heads in spring; pollen in early summer; seeds from brown heads in late summer; rootstalk throughout winter.

Preparation: Spring shoots are peeled, eaten raw or cooked. Spring heads are boiled and eaten in the same manner as corn-on-the-cob. Early summer pollen is gathered by shaking flower head gently into a container. Pollen is high in protein and can be mixed in baked goods. Late summer, before plant has gone to seed, small seeds from the heads can be harvested by burning the head, then winnowed. In winter the peeled rootstalk can be dried and pounded for flour.

Notes of Interest: A stand of Cattails will provide food, shelter and fuel for your fire; 3 of the 5 basic survival needs at any time of year.

0 mm	1 cm	2 cm	3 cm	4 cm	5 cm	6 cm	7 cm	8 cm	9 cm	1 dm 10 cm

1 mm = 0.04 inches   1 cm = 0.39 inches   1 dm = 3.94 inches   1 m = 39.37 inches

0 in.   1 in.   2 in.   3 in.   4 in.

Edible Plant

Ht: 2 m

CHICKWEED

Stellaria media / **CARYOPHYLLACEAE**   **Pink family**

Other Common Names: Starwort, *S. media:* Common Chickweed

Description: *Stellaria:* Leafy stems frequently branched; leaves oval (egg-shaped) or linear; flowers white in clusters or borne in angle between leaf and stem. *S. media:* Stems 5-45 cm long; leaves opposite, oval, smooth and pointed; flowers small, white, star-shaped, borne in stem-leaf angle. Flowers may not open when overcast or rainy.

Range: *Stellaria:* Distributed throughout North America in moist, shady, low elevations in waste or cultivated ground.

Season: Nearly entire year.

Edible: Young stems and leaves.

Preparation: Eaten raw or cooked. The tender, juicy stems are good in salads or in cooked vegetable dishes. When boiled like spinach, the flavor is quite mild, and the addition of some Shepherd's Purse, Wintercress or other flavor rich herb enhances the flavor. Plant also used for both hot and cold drinks.

Notes of Interest: Plant leaf is rich in iron. Because the plant is available most of the year, it provides a winter source of vitamin C while most other greens are unavailable.

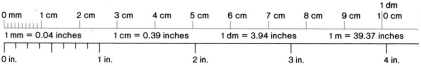

									1 dm
0 mm	1 cm	2 cm	3 cm	4 cm	5 cm	6 cm	7 cm	8 cm	9 cm 1 0 cm

1 mm = 0.04 inches   1 cm = 0.39 inches   1 dm = 3.94 inches   1 m = 39.37 inches

0 in.   1 in.   2 in.   3 in.   4 in.

Edible Plant

CHICORY

Cichorium intybus / **COMPOSITAE**   **Sunflower family**

Other Common Names: Blue Sailors, Wild Succory

Description: Erect, branching, perennial herb 5-17 dm tall; long, deep taproot; large clustered, coarsely toothed leaves growing from plant base in spreading rosette; upper leaves small; flower bright blue; flower heads up to 2.5 cm. Flowers usually close in bright sunlight.

Range: Widely distributed throughout North America; plains, waste places, piedmont valleys, open fields and roadsides.

Season: Primarily spring and summer.

Edible: In spring, entire plant; spring and early summer, greens; root, in all seasons.

Preparation: Relative of the dandelion, prepares in much the same way. In spring entire plant can be cut off just below rosette and used as potherb. Fresh, raw greens can be used for salads. Mature greens are better cooked. Roots can be dug any time, washed and roasted until they turn dark brown and snap easily. Roasted roots are ground and brewed like coffee, but makes much stronger brew than coffee beans.

Notes of Interest: Chicory was introduced from Europe. This plant is rich in vitamin A; also contains vitamin C.

0 mm	1 cm	2 cm	3 cm	4 cm	5 cm	6 cm	7 cm	8 cm	9 cm	1 dm 10 cm

1 mm = 0.04 inches   1 cm = 0.39 inches   1 dm = 3.94 inches   1 m = 39.37 inches

0 in.   1 in.   2 in.   3 in.   4 in.

Edible Plant

Ht: 12 dm

CHOCOLATE LILY

Fritillaria lanceolata / **LILIACEAE   Lily family**

Other Common Names: Rice Root Lily, Brown Lily, Indian Rice, Sour-dough Lily, Mission Bells

Description: *Fritillaria:* Perennial herbs with a simple erect stem 2-7 dm tall, from scaly bulbs surrounded by numerous rice-like bulblets; leaves alternate or in a circular arrangement, linear to lance-like; flowers single or few, usually large and showy, bell-shaped, nodding. *F. lanceolata:* Leaves are lance-shaped, mainly in 2 or 3 circular arrangements about the stem; purplish-colored flowers are mottled with greenish-yellow spots.

Range: *Fritillaria:* A widely varied habitat in the western United States and B.C., Canada. *F. lanceolata:* Open hillsides, prairies, grassy open woods, primarily in coastal regions.

Season: Blooms March through May.

Edible: Bulb.

Preparation: The bulb can be eaten raw, but is best cooked or steamed. Do not overcook as the bulb is tender and delicate and nearly rice-like in taste. Indians of the Northwest dried these bulbs and pounded them for flour.

Notes of Interest: Although *Fritillaria* is not an endangered plant species, it is among those we discourage the harvesting of for aesthetic reasons. The bulb of *F. meleagris,* a European species, is reported to be poisonous.

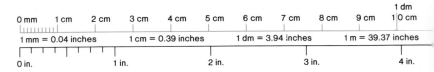

0 mm	1 cm	2 cm	3 cm	4 cm	5 cm	6 cm	7 cm	8 cm	9 cm	1 dm 10 cm

1 mm = 0.04 inches	1 cm = 0.39 inches	1 dm = 3.94 inches	1 m = 39.37 inches

0 in.	1 in.	2 in.	3 in.	4 in.

CHOKECHERRY

Prunus virginiana / **ROSACEAE** **Rose family**

Other Common Names: Wild Cherry, Stone-fruit, *P. virginiana:* Western Chokecherry

Description: *Prunus:* Deciduous shrub or small shrub-like tree 1-15 m tall; brown to reddish-brown bark; leaves simple and saw-toothed; flowers pink, red or white, single or clustered. *P. virginiana:* 2-8 m tall; leaves are oval to oblong-oval, tapering at ends, 4-9 cm; numerous creamy white flower clusters on long stem; mature, egg-shaped fruit is deep red to dark purple.

Range: *Prunus:* Throughout North America in open woods, on prairies, hillsides, canyonsides and stream banks.

Season: Blooms in May; fruit from late summer into autumn.

Edible: Primarily the autumn fruit.

Preparation: Fruit is edible raw; however, taste is quite sour, particularly if harvested before autumn. Drying or cooking tends to remove sourness. One method used to preserve fruit is by partially drying, then mashing and forming into cakes for final drying. These cakes can be stored and cooked before eating. Fruit makes delicious syrup and jelly or jam.

Notes of Interest: Leaves and pits of all species of *Prunus* contain cyanogenetic glycoside, a cyanide toxin which can be deadly, but which is so unstable that it is expelled by both drying and cooking.

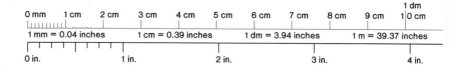

0 mm	1 cm	2 cm	3 cm	4 cm	5 cm	6 cm	7 cm	8 cm	9 cm	1 dm 10 cm

1 mm = 0.04 inches   1 cm = 0.39 inches   1 dm = 3.94 inches   1 m = 39.37 inches

0 in.	1 in.	2 in.	3 in.	4 in.

Edible Plant

Ht: 2.5 m

Prunus virginiana **Rose Family**

CLOVER

Trifolium pratense / **LEGUMINOSAE   Pea family**

Other Common Names: Red Clover

Description: *Trifolium:* Multiple stemmed base, perennial herb; leaves compound, 3 (occasionally more) leaflets; spike-like, clustered flower head. *T. pratense:* Branching stems 2-10 dm high with soft hairs; deep green leaflets, oval to oblong 2- 6 cm long; flower head is lavender to purple.

Range: *Trifolium:* Extensively throughout North America in a wide variety of moist habitats, and occasionally even in relatively dry ones.

Season: Primarily spring, summer and fall.

Edible: Flowers, leaves, roots and seeds.

Preparation: Although edible raw, it is difficult to digest unless cooked. Leaves and roots are boiled or steamed. Flowers and seeds are dried and used in baked goods or added to soups and stews. "Vine-dried" flower heads can be harvested in winter and steeped for tea.

Notes of Interest: *Trifolium* is high in protein. Medicinal applications include boiling flowers with equal proportions of water. Derived syrup is treatment for sore throat and cough. The color plate also includes *T. repense,* the common White Clover which is also edible.

| 0 mm | 1 cm | 2 cm | 3 cm | 4 cm | 5 cm | 6 cm | 7 cm | 8 cm | 9 cm | 1 dm 10 cm |

1 mm = 0.04 inches   1 cm = 0.39 inches   1 dm = 3.94 inches   1 m = 39.37 inches

| 0 in. | 1 in. | 2 in. | 3 in. | 4 in. |

Edible Plant

Ht: 2 dm

COLTSFOOT

Petasites frigidus / **COMPOSITAE**   **Composite family**

Other Common Names: Alpine Coltsfoot

Description: *Petasites:* Stout perennial herb to 7 dm tall; broad basal leaves, toothed and mostly deeply cleft, woolly underside, with stem leaves reduced to encircling modified leaf form; white to pale-purple flower head, small, many flowers in soft loose cluster, on ends of scaly stalks. *P. frigidus:* Stems from rootstalk are branching 15-20 cm high with few encircling modified leaves; leaves broadly triangular in outline; 5-10 white flower heads each at the end of a stout stem.

Range: *Petasites:* Frequently found in moist woods and in clusters along stream banks. *F. frigidus:* Found at higher altitudes in the northern Cascades.

Season: Blooms frequently before leaves appear in early spring following retreating snow. Edible in spring and summer.

Edible: Early leaves and flowers.

Preparation: Although the young leaves and flowers make an excellent potherb, the most unique quality of the plant is that it is a source for a salt substitute. The stems and leaves are allowed to wilt and dry, then are rolled in tight balls and reduced to an ashen consistency by burning over coals or encasing in a ball of clay and firing.

Notes of Interest: *Tussilago farfara,* a plant which is similar to *P. frigidus* also shares the common name, Coltsfoot. Its leaves are round and flowers are many-rayed.

0 mm	1 cm	2 cm	3 cm	4 cm	5 cm	6 cm	7 cm	8 cm	9 cm	1 dm 10 cm

1 mm = 0.04 inches	1 cm = 0.39 inches	1 dm = 3.94 inches	1 m = 39.37 inches

0 in.	1 in.	2 in.	3 in.	4 in.

Edible Plant

Ht: 6 dm

COW PARSNIP

Heracleum lanatum / **UMBELLIFERAE   Parsley family**

Other Common Names: Wild Parsnip, Wild Rhubarb

Description: Single-stemmed perennial 1-3 m tall; leaves once ternate with broad, distinctly stalked, coarsely toothed, and palmately lobed leaflets; leaflets 1-4 dm long and wide; stems and leaves usually with hairs; flowers white, borne in compound umbels, the terminal umbel 1-2 dm wide; fruit obovate to obcordate, 7-12 mm long x 5-9 mm wide. Crushed tissue has aromatic, somewhat unpleasant, parsnip-like odor.

Range: Widespread in North America.

Season: Spring, summer and fall when leaves are present for identification.

Edible: Root, flowering stems, leafstalks.

Preparation: Young leafstalks and stems gathered before flower clusters mature, are stewed. When flower stems are 3-4 cm across, but prior to flowering, tender stems are cut into short pieces and boiled twice (discarding the first water), and stewed like celery. Root is dug, washed and cooked.

Notes of Interest: Care should be taken in making positive identification. This plant can, at certain times, bear a resemblance to Water Hemlock which is deadly poisonous. When Cow Parsnip is in leaf, it is unmistakable due to the very large leaf size.

0 mm	1 cm	2 cm	3 cm	4 cm	5 cm	6 cm	7 cm	8 cm	9 cm	1 dm 10 cm

1 mm = 0.04 inches	1 cm = 0.39 inches	1 dm = 3.94 inches	1 m = 39.37 inches

0 in.	1 in.	2 in.	3 in.	4 in.

Edible Plant

Ht: 1.5 m

Heracleum lanatum **Parsley Family**

CURRANT

Ribes inerme / **SAXIFRAGACEAE**   **Saxifrage family**

Other Common Names: Gooseberry, Squaw Currant, Bear Currant, *R. inerme:* White-stemmed Currant

Description: *Ribes:* Vertical shrubs with or without spines 6 dm to 7 m tall; leaves alternate, small, maple-like leaf shape; berries range in color from bright red to black, with currant berry smooth, while gooseberry is extremely rough or prickly; flowers grow singly or in clusters. *R. inerme:* Stems 1-2 m high; whitish bark; leaves cleft or coarsely toothed; flowers, 1-3 borne on leaf axis are white; berries, dark red.

Range: *Ribes:* North America in a variety of habitats; inclined to be found in moist mountain soil or along dry creekbeds, springs or other likely source of underground water.

Season: Early leafing, blooming in late March through May; fruit by late summer and fall.

Edible: Berries of all species.

Preparation: Berries eaten raw, cooked or sun-dried. Berries are not succulent and vary in taste from sour to tart to sweet. *Ribes* can be cooked in baked goods and make excellent preserves.

Notes of Interest: Indians of the West used this berry as an ingredient for pemmican. Eating raw berries in quantity can act as an emetic. The species name, *R. inerme,* is a misname in that *inerme,* which means "unarmed" is inappropriate since the stems have both spines and prickles.

0 mm	1 cm	2 cm	3 cm	4 cm	5 cm	6 cm	7 cm	8 cm	9 cm	1 dm 10 cm

1 mm = 0.04 inches	1 cm = 0.39 inches	1 dm = 3.94 inches	1 m = 39.37 inches

0 in.	1 in.	2 in.	3 in.	4 in.

DANDELION

Taraxacum officinale / **COMPOSITAE** **Sunflower family**

Other Common Names: Common Dandelion, Blowball

Description: Perennial or biennial herb with hollow, leafless stem, 5-50 cm tall; thin, deep green, coarsely toothed, clustered leaves growing from plant base in spreading rosette; long, thick taproot; each stem has a single flower head or seed head; flower bright yellow; seed heads are white.

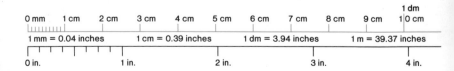

Range: Abundant throughout North America; open fields, roadsides and lawns.

Season: Blossoms in early spring through summer; edibles, spring through fall.

Edible: Leaves and root.

Preparation: Young leaves harvested before flowers appear can be used in salads or cooked like domestic greens. Should the taste be too bitter a change of cooking water will remove the bitterness. Roots are best dug in autumn and should be dried uncut until hard. Like Chicory root, dried roots are slowly roasted and ground as a coffee substitute.

Notes of Interest: Superior source of vitamins, containing a large amount of vitamin A, also B, C, and E. Dandelion greens are rated very high nutritionally.

0 mm	1 cm	2 cm	3 cm	4 cm	5 cm	6 cm	7 cm	8 cm	9 cm	1 dm 10 cm

1 mm = 0.04 inches	1 cm = 0.39 inches	1 dm = 3.94 inches	1 m = 39.37 inches

0 in.	1 in.	2 in.	3 in.	4 in.

Edible Plant

Ht: 2 dm

DAY LILY

Hemerocallis fulva / **LILIACEAE   Lily family**

Other Common Names: Tawny Day Lily

Description: *Hemerocallis:* Showy perennial herbs from fleshy-fibrous roots or tubers; keeled leaves long and linear at base of tall naked flowering stem; large yellow to reddish-yellow flowers, withers and decays after blooming for a single day. *H. fulva:* Leaves 1-2 cm broad; flowering stem 5-20 dm high, 3-15 flowered; wavy-edged flowers are orange, deepening in color toward center.

Range: *Hemerocallis:* In colonies or clumps along ditches and roadsides in damp soil. *H. fulva:* Western United States. *H. flava:* Primarily found in the northeastern United States west to Michigan.

Season: Blooms May through July.

Edible: Buds, flowers, tubers.

Preparation: The buds and flowers, long a standard vegetable in the Orient, have many uses in cookery. Care should be taken not to overcook the flower buds. Boil only a few minutes when prepared as a solo dish topped with butter. Buds and flowers can both be added to soup or stew a few minutes before removing from heat. The early tubers are good and crisp in a salad, or eaten raw alone.

Notes of Interest: *Hemerocallis* was originally a cultivated flower but easily escaped cultivation. They are hearty and thrive when thinned. *Hemerocallis* is Greek literally meaning "beautiful for a day," hence its common name, Day Lily, is derived.

0 mm	1 cm	2 cm	3 cm	4 cm	5 cm	6 cm	7 cm	8 cm	9 cm	1 dm 10 cm

1 mm = 0.04 inches   1 cm = 0.39 inches   1 dm = 3.94 inches   1 m = 39.37 inches

0 in.	1 in.	2 in.	3 in.	4 in.

Edible Plant

Ht: 6 dm

DOCK

Rumex crispus / **POLYGONACEAE** **Buckwheat family**

Other Common Names: Dock, Yellow Dock, *R. crispus:* Curly-leaved Dock

Description: *Rumex:* Perennial, and occasionally annual, stout-stemmed, herb 1 dm to 2.5 m tall; often large, alternate, basal leaves. *R. crispus:* Stem 4-12 dm tall; leaves very wavy-edged and blue-green in color; plant supports tall flower spike containing numerous, small flowers in long, narrow clusters which are variations of green; fruit has pronounced veins and is roughly triangular-heart-shaped, 4-5 mm.

Range: *Rumex:* Abundant throughout much of North America; grows in fields, cultivated ground and piedmont valleys.

Season: Edible primarily in spring and fall.

Edible: Leaves.

Preparation: Leaves should be harvested when young and served as cooked greens. If leaves are bitter, cook in two or more changes of water.

Notes of Interest: Dock leaves are rich in vitamins A and C, containing more vitamin A than carrots. Dye was extracted from the root by the Navaho Indians. Dock is also a medicinal herb listed in the *U.S. Dispensary.*

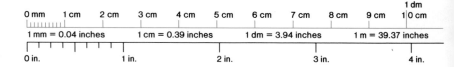

0 mm	1 cm	2 cm	3 cm	4 cm	5 cm	6 cm	7 cm	8 cm	9 cm	1 dm 10 cm

1 mm = 0.04 inches   1 cm = 0.39 inches   1 dm = 3.94 inches   1 m = 39.37 inches

0 in.	1 in.	2 in.	3 in.	4 in.

Edible Plant

Ht: 6 dm

EVENING PRIMROSE

Oenothera biennis / **ONAGRACEAE**   **Evening Primrose family**

Other Common Names: Common Evening Primrose

Description: *Oenothera:* Annual, biennial or perennial herb with or without elongated leaf-bearing stem; leaves alternate or basal; 4-petaled flowers yellow or white becoming reddish or purplish with age. *O. biennis:* Biennial or short-lived perennial; stems reddish, erect, stout, hairy, usually simple, 5-12 dm high; numerous leaves are lance-like to lance-oblong 4-20 cm long; flowers in modified leaf spike; petals broadly inversely oval and light yellow in color.

Range: *Oenothera:* Found throughout much of the United States and Canada. *O. biennis:* In moist open meadows near coniferous forests and in sandy ground west of the Cascades to British Columbia and in Newfoundland and New York. 1000-1300 m elevation.

Season: Varies spring to fall.

Edible: The root is the primary edible and is best harvested before the plant flowers.

Preparation: The root is best peeled and boiled and is quite nutritious if it can be harvested at a time when the root is not too peppery. Generally, the most palatable time is early spring, but this varies to such an extent that sometimes the plant is mildest in the fall. If the root proves too peppery a second boiling may be necessary.

Notes of Interest: There are many species within *Oenothera* which are edible, however, the genus is extremely varied, and hybridizes so easily and readily that it is difficult to make a generalized statement about edibility of all species.

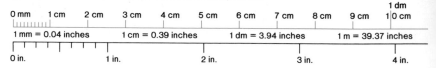

0 mm	1 cm	2 cm	3 cm	4 cm	5 cm	6 cm	7 cm	8 cm	9 cm	1 dm / 10 cm

1 mm = 0.04 inches   1 cm = 0.39 inches   1 dm = 3.94 inches   1 m = 39.37 inches

0 in.	1 in.	2 in.	3 in.	4 in.

BLUE ELDERBERRY

Sambucus caerulea / **CAPRIFOLIACEAE   Honeysuckle family**

Other Common Names: Elder, Blue-berried Elder

Description: Pithy stemmed, deciduous shrub or tree, 2-8 m tall; compound leaves divided
into opposing, serrate-edged leaflets. *S. caerulea:*
Large, flat-topped clusters of very small, cream to white
colored flowers; berry-like fruit is powdery blue.

Range: Found in moist, subalpine areas throughout
North America.

Season: Blooms in June at most elevations; produces
berries in autumn.

Edible: Fruit (berry) and flower.

Preparation: Sweet, juicy berry is edible raw or cooked.
Flowers dipped in batter and fried are a pleasant dish.
Both berries and blossoms can be steeped in water for a
hot drink. There are a large variety of ways to use the berries including preserves, sauces, pies and Elderberry wine.

Notes of Interest: Berries are a rich source of vitamins A and C. This plant is considered
nature's medicine chest. Among other remedies, the leaf can be mashed with the fingers
until the green chlorophyll juice can be applied to poison oak. The raw berries of the Red
Elderberry (*S. racemosa*) should be considered toxic. *S. racemosa* is described in the Poisonous Plant section.

0 mm	1 cm	2 cm	3 cm	4 cm	5 cm	6 cm	7 cm	8 cm	9 cm	1 dm 10 cm

1 mm = 0.04 inches   1 cm = 0.39 inches   1 dm = 3.94 inches   1 m = 39.37 inches

0 in.	1 in.	2 in.	3 in.	4 in.

Edible Plant

FIREWEED

Epilobium angustifolium / **ONAGRACEAE** **Evening Primrose family**

Other Common Names: Great Willow Herb

Description: Erect stemmed perennial 1-2 m tall; long, fairly slender, deep green, minutely toothed and alternating leaves; tall stem bears a spire of bright magenta (wine-colored) flowers.

Range: Temperate North America; frequently found in logged and burned areas or in moist soil of open woods or along streams.

Season: Blooms nearly all summer; edible during spring sprouting season.

Edible: Young shoots and leaves; flower buds.

Preparation: Young shoots, leaves and the budded stem tips are eaten raw or cooked. Stem pith is good raw, dried or boiled; fine in soups or stews. Tea is made from either green or dried leaves.

Notes of Interest: In late summer the seed pods split into quarters, curling back in large, loose spirals to release fluffy, hairy, cotton-like material which is excellent for fire starting or used for insulation. The name given this plant is indicative of where it is frequently seen growing, in burn areas.

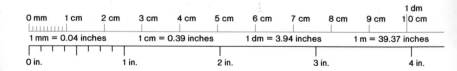

0 mm	1 cm	2 cm	3 cm	4 cm	5 cm	6 cm	7 cm	8 cm	9 cm	1 dm 10 cm

1 mm = 0.04 inches   1 cm = 0.39 inches   1 dm = 3.94 inches   1 m = 39.37 inches

0 in.	1 in.	2 in.	3 in.	4 in.

GREEN GENTIAN

Frasera speciosa / **GENTIANACEAE**   **Gentian family**

Other Common Names: Giant Swertia, Deer Tongue, Elkweed

Description: *Frasera:* Mostly perennial herbs from a stout, fleshy taproot; stems 3 dm to 2 m tall from basal rosette of long, smooth leaves; stem leaves whorled; numerous flowers on 1 or more short stalks; flower color varies from bluish-purple to white or green. *F. speciosa:* Single, stout, coarse, erect, unbranched flowering stem 5-20 dm high; oblong lance-like basal leaves dense with the larger ones nearest the base; stem leaves much smaller, whorled 3 to 5; numerous flowers borne on long stalk are greenish-white with specks of purple.

Range: Scattered throughout the western United States in medium-dry open areas mostly above 1200 m and occur to 3000 m.

Season: Flowers in June through early August depending upon the species and elevation.

Edible: The taproot.

Preparation: This fleshy taproot, which was another of the roots in the diet of the Indians of the West, may be eaten raw, roasted, or boiled. The root can be sliced carrot fashion and prepared with other potherbs.

Notes of Interest: The roots of some species are used medicinally, including use as an emetic and cathartic. The root of *F. speciosa* however, will not affect the digestive system when consumed in normal quantities.

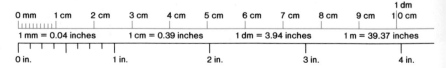

0 mm	1 cm	2 cm	3 cm	4 cm	5 cm	6 cm	7 cm	8 cm	9 cm	1 dm 10 cm

1 mm = 0.04 inches   1 cm = 0.39 inches   1 dm = 3.94 inches   1 m = 39.37 inches

0 in.   1 in.   2 in.   3 in.   4 in.

 **Edible Plant**

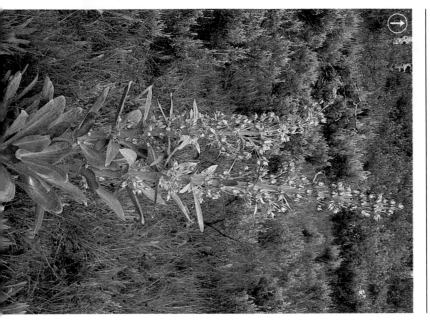

GROUND-CHERRY

Physalis longifolia / **SOLANACEAE** **Nightshade family**

Other Common Names: Husk Tomato, Strawberry Tomato

Description: *Physalis:* Sprawling perennial or annual herbs, branches single or forked, frequently covering more than 1 sq m of ground; lance-like leaves, single, edges smooth or serrate; flowers mostly singular, spring from axil; fruit, seeded berry is inflated and 5-angled or prominently 10-ribbed. *P. longifolia:* Leaves thick, lance-like, leafstalk 1-3 cm long; floral envelope segments are triangular; fruiting floral envelope is spherical to oval, slightly sunken at base, 3-3.5 cm long, loosely encasing the sticky yellow berry.

Range: *Physalis:* Frequently found in recently cultivated fields and open ground in moist to medium dry soil in many areas from the Atlantic to the Pacific.

Season: Flowers appear in June to mid-July. The fruit ripens in late July through September.

Edible: Mature berries.

Preparation: The berries frequently fall to the ground before they are fully ripe. Allow them to ripen in the husk where they become sweeter and the encased berry will store for weeks. The soft and sweet berry can be eaten raw or cooked, or made into jam, syrup and pies. Husked and served with honey and cream these berries make a splendid dessert.

Notes of Interest: The Ground-Cherry belongs to the Nightshade family and is closely related to the tomato.

0 mm	1 cm	2 cm	3 cm	4 cm	5 cm	6 cm	7 cm	8 cm	9 cm	1 dm 1 0 cm

1 mm = 0.04 inches   1 cm = 0.39 inches   1 dm = 3.94 inches   1 m = 39.37 inches

0 in.	1 in.	2 in.	3 in.	4 in.

Edible Plant

HAZELNUT

Corylus cornuta / **CORYLACEAE**   **Hazel family**

Other Common Names: Beaked Hazelnut, Filbert, *C. cornuta:* Western Hazelnut

Description: *Corylus:* Smooth, brownish barked shrub or small tree 2-10 m tall; simple, alternate, round to oval, pointed tip, deciduous leaves 5-15 cm long; flowers clustered; brown oval fruit (nut) is wrapped in pale green, bristly, sheath-like husk which turns light brown as nut ripens. *C. cornuta:* Tall shrub, maximum 5 m high; fruit, 1-2; flowers appear long before leaves.

Range: *Corylus:* One species or another widely distributed over North America; edges of clearings and along stream banks.

Season: Late summer and into the fall, as late as October.

Edible: Nut.

Preparation: It is usually easiest to shake bush and then pick up fallen nuts which will often still be in the husks. Watch for small holes in the shells as you husk the nuts. These holes indicate that worms have entered and destroyed the fruit. Hulled and shelled nuts can be eaten raw, roasted, or ground for meal. In their shells nuts can be stored for long periods of time, provided they are dry.

Notes of Interest: Cracked shells make excellent kindling material for a cooking fire. The two European hazels *(Corylus avellana pontica* and *C. maxima)* are commercially sold as "filberts."

0 mm	1 cm	2 cm	3 cm	4 cm	5 cm	6 cm	7 cm	8 cm	9 cm	1 dm 10 cm

1 mm = 0.04 inches	1 cm = 0.39 inches	1 dm = 3.94 inches	1 m = 39.37 inches

0 in.	1 in.	2 in.	3 in.	4 in.

HIGH-BUSH CRANBERRY

Viburnum edule / **CAPRIFOLIACEAE** **Honeysuckle family**

Other Common Names: Arrowwood, Squawbush

Description: *Viburnum:* Slender shrubs or shrubby tree 1-4.5 m high; leaves opposite, lobed and toothed; flower cluster is borne in between opposing leaves. *V. edule:* Several stems 1-3 m tall; buds and white flowers mostly upright, but droop as they mature into bright red berries. The drawing illustrates the plant in the budding stage.

Range: *Viburnum:* Throughout northern United States and Canada; in woods, thickets, bogs and along mountain streams.

Season: Blooms in spring and early summer; fruit in fall and winter.

Edible: Berry.

Preparation: Berry can be eaten raw, cooked or dried. Not related to cultivated cranberry, but when cooked, substitute for cranberry sauce. Pleasant, colorful drink is made by allowing berries to simmer, then mash, straining out seeds and skins. Add water to taste; serve hot or cold. Berries used in preserves, pies and even wine.

Notes of Interest: Berry is an excellent source of vitamin C. The name, Squawbush, apparently given for medicinal property of bark, which was used as a uterine sedative to quell menstrual pains by North American Indians.

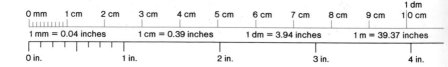

0 mm	1 cm	2 cm	3 cm	4 cm	5 cm	6 cm	7 cm	8 cm	9 cm	1 dm 10 cm
1 mm = 0.04 inches		1 cm = 0.39 inches			1 dm = 3.94 inches				1 m = 39.37 inches	

0 in.		1 in.		2 in.		3 in.		4 in.

Edible Plant

Ht: 3 m

HONEYSUCKLE

Lonicera involucrata / **CAPRIFOLIACEAE   Honeysuckle family**

Other Common Names: Honeysuckle Twinberry, Black Twinberry, Inkberry

Description: *Lonicera:* Erect or climbing, bushy shrub 3 dm to 6 m high; leaves opposite, simple; flowers in pairs or small clusters. *L. involucrata:* Erect, bushy shrub, 1-3 m tall; leaves oblong, smooth above and slightly hairy beneath; 2-3 times longer than wide, coming to a point on both ends; leaf edge fringed with short hairs; light yellow flowers in pairs on a common stalk between leaf and stem; fruit is black.

Range: *Lonicera:* Throughout North America as far southeast as Texas, growing in moist soil in thickets along streams as well as in open coniferous forests. One species, *L. caerulea,* is found up to 2700 m.

Season: Blooming period is May through July depending upon species; fruit is available in autumn.

Edible: Berry.

Preparation: Mature berries are good raw or dried.

Notes of Interest: Several species are toxic. *L. tartarica,* a native of Siberia and *L. xylosteum,* a native of Eastern Eurasia are repulsively bitter and are a purgative.

0 mm	1 cm	2 cm	3 cm	4 cm	5 cm	6 cm	7 cm	8 cm	9 cm	1 dm / 10 cm

1 mm = 0.04 inches   1 cm = 0.39 inches   1 dm = 3.94 inches   1 m = 39.37 inches

0 in.	1 in.	2 in.	3 in.	4 in.

Edible Plant

Ht: 12 dm

Lonicera involucrata **Honeysuckle Family**

HORSETAIL

Equisetum arvense / **EQUISETACEAE** **Horsetail family**

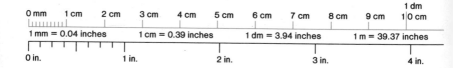

Other Common Names: Scouring Rush, *E. arvense:* Common Horsetail

Description: *Equisetum:* Annual or perennial, rush-like plant 5 cm to 15 dm high; creeping, mostly hollow, stems with long, rounded grooves and without green foliage; branches simple or in circular array. *E. arvense:* Silica covered, stemmed perennial 5-30 cm high; fertile plant stems simple, erect, short-lived; sheaths loose, pale with 8-12 brown lance-like teeth; cylindric spike 2-3 cm long; sterile plant is 1-6 dm long, erect or ascending with slender branches in a dense circular array.

Range: *Equisetum:* Widely distributed throughout North America; moist places, swampy areas, sandy stream banks.

Season: Fertile stems appear in early spring followed by edible sterile stems.

Edible: Young shoots and stem pulp.

Preparation: Young shoots are usable as a potherb, however mature stems are quite stiff and contain silica. At this stage the tough outer tissue of the stem can be peeled, exposing a sweet pulpy material which is eaten raw.

Notes of Interest: The siliconed stems were used by the early American settlers for scouring pots and pans. This plant has poisoned livestock, but is apparently harmless to humans in small or moderate quantities.

										1 dm
0 mm	1 cm	2 cm	3 cm	4 cm	5 cm	6 cm	7 cm	8 cm	9 cm	10 cm

1 mm = 0.04 inches   1 cm = 0.39 inches   1 dm = 3.94 inches   1 m = 39.37 inches

0 in.	1 in.	2 in.	3 in.	4 in.

Edible Plant

Ht: 3 dm

HUCKLEBERRY

Vaccinium ovalifolium / **ERICACEAE**   **Heath family**

Other Common Names: Blueberry

Description: *Vaccinium:* Small vine-like to large, sturdy, evergreen or deciduous, erect or depressed shrubs 5 cm to 3 m tall; leaves simple and alternate. *V. ovalifolium:* Relatively tall shrub 1-3 m tall; branches slender and sharply angled; leaves oval, thin, whitish powder beneath; single flower at stem-leaf junction is mostly pink; berry is deep blue and powdered 7-9 mm in diameter. The drawing is of *V. parvifolium:* the Red Huckleberry.

Range: *Vaccinium:* Northern United States and California, Canada and Alaska; in a variety of habitats from bogs to dry mountain slopes, depending upon species.

Season: Blooming period, May and June; fruit ripens in July to September.

Edible: Berry.

Preparation: Most berries are succulent, excellent raw, but can be cooked or dried. These delicious berries make fine preserves and are good in baked dishes. Refreshing cold drink is made by diluting berry juice with water. Hot drinks are best made from the dried berry.

Notes of Interest: Huckleberry fruit is a source of vitamins A, B[1] and C with traces of calcium, phosphorous and iron.

| 0 mm | 1 cm | 2 cm | 3 cm | 4 cm | 5 cm | 6 cm | 7 cm | 8 cm | 9 cm | 1 dm
1 0 cm |

1 mm = 0.04 inches   1 cm = 0.39 inches   1 dm = 3.94 inches   1 m = 39.37 inches

| 0 in. | 1 in. | 2 in. | 3 in. | 4 in. |

Edible Plant

Ht: 12 dm

INDIAN POTATO

Orogenia fusiformis / **UMBELLIFERAE**   **Parsley family**

Other Common Names: Indian Potato, Snowdrops, Mountain Orogenia

Description: *Orogenia:* Small, delicate, perennial with fleshy roots and stems mostly below ground and sheathed with bladeless modified leaf structure; leaves are in 3s and in narrow linear segments; the flower head is a small imperfectly compound umbrella shape with few unequal rays; flower petals are white. *O. fusiformis:* Small perennial without hairs, 5-15 cm high; fleshy root is spindle or carrot-shaped, with base enclosed by a pair of purplish papery sheaths; leaves as described in genus, 1-4 cm long; flower head contains 3-12 unequal rays.

Range: Found in rich moist soil of mountain valleys and slopes in the western United States above 1500 m with the exception of Arizona and New Mexico.

Season: Flowers in April and May, blooming as soon as the snow melts.

Edible: The tuber-like root.

Preparation: The roots of *O. fusiformis* and *O. linearifolia* are eaten raw, roasted, fried, or baked. They have a potato-like taste and were part of the Indian diet, hence the common name, Indian Potato.

Notes of Interest: This plant is one of the earliest spring flowers to appear in the higher mountain slopes and valleys, emerging through melting banks of snow.

0 mm	1 cm	2 cm	3 cm	4 cm	5 cm	6 cm	7 cm	8 cm	9 cm	1 dm 10 cm

1 mm = 0.04 inches   1 cm = 0.39 inches   1 dm = 3.94 inches   1 m = 39.37 inches

| 0 in. | 1 in. | 2 in. | 3 in. | 4 in. |

Edible Plant

Ht: 9 cm

INDIAN RHUBARB

Peltiphyllum peltatum / **SAXIFRAGACEAE   Saxifrage family**

Other Common Names: Shieldleaf, Umbrella-plant

Description: Large coarse perennial herb 4-13 dm high; with stout spreading rootstalks; the slightly cupped or depressed center leaves are all basal, shield-shaped 2-5 dm wide, 9-12 lobes, the primary lobes divided into secondary lobes, giving a coarsely toothed appearance; thick fleshy leaf stems 6-12 dm support leaves; flower heads are large and open, flowers are in a branched, single row arrangement; petals are white, 6-8 mm long.

Range: Found along mountain streams in southern Oregon and northern California to 1500 m.

Season: Blooms in early spring; normally the flowers have wilted well before the appearance of the leaves.

Edible: Fleshy leafstalk, and young leaf.

Preparation: The thick fleshy leafstalks of the young plant are peeled and eaten raw. Cut sections can be added to stews or cooked as a potherb.

Notes of Interest: The plant was selected in spite of its extremely limited range because *P. peltatum* and its immediate environment (as pictured in the color plate) epitomize the beauty and harmony of an untouched virgin wilderness. The photo portrays a rare state of this plant, a time when both flowers and leaves are present.

| 0 mm | 1 cm | 2 cm | 3 cm | 4 cm | 5 cm | 6 cm | 7 cm | 8 cm | 9 cm | 1 dm 10 cm |

1 mm = 0.04 inches   1 cm = 0.39 inches   1 dm = 3.94 inches   1 m = 39.37 inches

| 0 in. | 1 in. | 2 in. | 3 in. | 4 in. |

Edible Plant

Ht: 10 dm

Peltiphyllum peltatum **Saxifrage Family**

KINNIKINNICK

Arctostaphylos uva-ursi / **ERICACEAE Heath family**

Other Common Names: Bearberry, Manzanita, Kinnikinic (alternate spelling)

Description: *Arctostaphylos:* Evergreen shrub, 1 dm to 3 m high; smooth, polished, reddish-brown bark; simple leaves. *A. uva-ursi:* Dense shrub, 1-4 dm high; stems long, creeping; leaves leathery and bright, shiny green to gray-green; flowers are waxy, white to pink, dense clusters, urn or bell shaped; berry bright red.

Range: *Arctostaphylos:* Throughout foothills and mountains of northern United States and southern Canada; generally found in the shade along the edge of coniferous forests.

Season: Blooms in spring; bears food from late summer through winter.

Edible: Berry is primary food source.

Preparation: Ripe berries are eaten raw or cooked and chilled. Refreshing "Kink-drink" made by scalding and mashing ripe berries. Add water and allow to chill.

Notes of Interest: Berries are rich in vitamin C and are tart-sweet in taste. Indians and old-timers have crushed the dry leaves for smoking. Leaves contain high concentration of tannin which can be processed and used for tanning, dyeing, and medicinally.

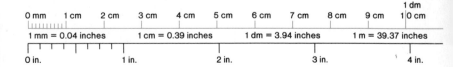

LAMB'S-QUARTERS

Chenopodium album / **CHENOPODIACEAE** Pigweed family

Other Common Names: Pigweed, Goosefoot, Wild Spinach

Description: *Chenopodium:* Annual or perennial, succulent, herb, 1-15 dm high; leaves alternate, frequently mealy or powdery, particularly on leaf underside; inconspicuous flowers are green, arranged in spikes or small dense clusters. *C. album:* Erect, branching-stemmed herb, 1-12 dm high; branches ascending; leaves roughly egg-shaped but wedge-shaped at base and quite pointed at tip; pronounced veins, leaf edges toothed; flowers in narrow spikes.

Range: *Chenopodium:* Cultivated ground throughout temperate North America.

Season: Appears in spring; becomes abundant mid to late summer.

Edible: Leaves and seeds.

Preparation: Young plants harvested as a potherb or as a salad base. Newer leaves from plant top can be picked throughout the summer and prepared like spinach. Ripe seeds are stripped from the plant, rubbed, winnowed and either boiled for mush or ground for flour.

Notes of Interest: This relative of spinach is the mildest flavored of all wild potherbs. The leaves are an excellent source of vitamins A and C. Some species have been used medicinally as a poultice to reduce swelling.

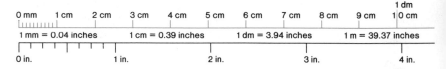

| 0 mm | 1 cm | 2 cm | 3 cm | 4 cm | 5 cm | 6 cm | 7 cm | 8 cm | 9 cm | 1 dm 10 cm |

1 mm = 0.04 inches   1 cm = 0.39 inches   1 dm = 3.94 inches   1 m = 39.37 inches

| 0 in. | 1 in. | 2 in. | 3 in. | 4 in. |

MAPLE

Acer macrophyllum / **ACERACEAE**   **Maple family**

Other Common Names: *A. macrophyllum:* Large-leaved Maple

Description: *Acer:* Shrubs or trees reaching 30 m height; leaves opposite and mostly palmately lobed; flowers clustered, small, drooping; fruit twin single seeds, long winged, splitting at maturity. *A. macrophyllum:* Large tree up to 30 m high; branches, large and long; leaves circular in outline, palmately lobed, coarsely toothed, up to 3 dm wide; flowers in dense cylinder-like clusters, yellow-green in color.

Range: *Acer:* Throughout temperate North America with *A. macrophyllum* and *A. grandidentatum* predominant in the West and *A. saccharum* in the East; in valleys, hillsides up to 2200 m.

Season: Provides edibles year-round; sap tapping in late winter or early spring; seed in fall.

Preparation: Seeds are edible raw or roasted. To obtain sap from *A. saccharum* drill a hole in the tree 2-3 cm deep, insert a tapping tube, and suspend a container from a nail below tube to collect sweet, thin, nutritious sap. Boil, spooning off scum, until a clear amber syrup is all that remains.

Notes of Interest: Maple sugar is more nutritious than its manufactured counterpart, containing the B vitamins, calcium and phosphorus.

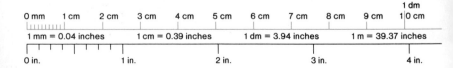

| 0 mm | 1 cm | 2 cm | 3 cm | 4 cm | 5 cm | 6 cm | 7 cm | 8 cm | 9 cm | 1 dm 10 cm |

1 mm = 0.04 inches   1 cm = 0.39 inches   1 dm = 3.94 inches   1 m = 39.37 inches

0 in.   1 in.   2 in.   3 in.   4 in.

MINER'S LETTUCE

Montia perfoliata / **PORTULACACEAE** **Purslane family**

Other Common Names: Indian Lettuce

Description: *Montia:* Succulent, small, annual or perennial herb 2 cm to 5 dm high; leaves basal, opposite or alternate; flowers borne along stem or in umbrella-like array. *M. perfoliata:* Annual herb up to 4 dm high; numerous basal stems; basal leaves, broad at base and narrowing abruptly; upper stem leaves united pair, disc-shaped and below flowers; flowers along stem are white-pink.

Range: *Montia:* Throughout much of North America; moist, shady ground, shaded stream banks.

Season: Blooms in April and May; edible from spring to fall.

Edible: Stems, leaves and roots.

Preparation: Leaves and stems are eaten raw. Excellent mixed with Watercress and used as a salad. Although plant can be cooked, it is much more nutritious raw. Roots are also edible raw, but good boiled. Gourmet treat: Rainbow trout, hot or chilled, with Miner's Lettuce and Watercress served between slices of root flour bread.

Notes of Interest: *M. perfoliata* was prized by the miners of the California Gold Rush as it substituted adequately for garden grown greens without the gardening hassle the miners had little or no time for anyway.

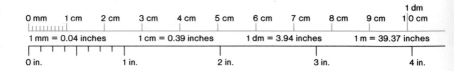

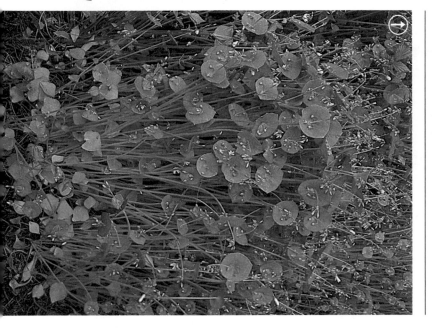

MOUNTAIN ASH

Sorbus scopulina / **ROSACEAE   Rose family**

Other Common Names: Rowan Tree

Description: *Sorbus:* Shrub or small trees with compound leaves and sharply indented leaflets borne along the axis; small flowers in large terminal compound flat-topped clusters; petals 5, white; fruit, a fleshy, but small, red or orange berry. *S. scopulina:* Shrub 1-7 m tall; early growth is grayish; leaflets usually 7 to 11, narrowly oblong-oval to oblong-lance-like, 2-9 cm long, edges finely sawtoothed, leaf surface dark green above and pale below; numerous white flowers in flower cluster; fruit, 1 cm diameter is orange to scarlet.

Range: *Sorbus:* Found primarily in moist middle elevation soils of mountainous areas of the northern hemisphere, from 1500 to 2200 m.

Season: Flowers May through July depending on the elevation and species. Berries edible in autumn.

Edible: The berries in early season are much too bitter to be eaten. However, when thoroughly ripe, and particularly following the first frost, the berries can be eaten raw, cooked, or even dried.

Notes of Interest: Pioneers used this berry in a variety of ways, including jam, pies and a somewhat bitter wine. *Sorbus* is a source of vitamin C.

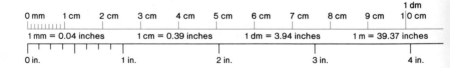

 **Edible Plant**

Ht: 4 m

MOUNTAIN DANDELION

Agoseris aurantiaca / **COMPOSITAE   Sunflower family**

Other Common Names: Goat Chicory, Slender Agoseris, Burnt-orange Agoseris

Description: *Agoseris:* Similar to the common dandelion *(Taraxacum officinale)* with hollow, nearly hairless, leafless stem 1-4 dm high; leaves, long, lance-like or narrowing gradually from summit, form a basal rosette, flowering head, singular, orange to reddish. *A. aurantiaca:* Characterized by slender seed beaks, and burnt-orange flowers. Species determination among *Agoseris* is difficult for the novice.

Range: Throughout Rocky Mountain region in dry to moist open woods and meadows above 2000 m.

Season: Blooms May through August depending upon elevation.

Edible: Leaves and roots.

Preparation: The leaves should be boiled before eating. The roots are edible raw, but are better boiled. Because *A. aurantiaca* is a much smaller plant than *T. officinale,* particularly the leafy part, it requires several times the amount of harvest to appreciate the same bulk and food value.

Notes of Interest: Like the common dandelion, when the stem or root tissue is broken, a milky juice escapes. Upon exposure to the air this sap turns quite thick and darkens in color. Although not of commercial value, this substance contains a small amount of rubber. This hardened sap was used as chewing gum by Indians of the West.

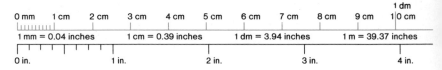

									1 dm
0 mm	1 cm	2 cm	3 cm	4 cm	5 cm	6 cm	7 cm	8 cm	9 cm 1 0 cm

1 mm = 0.04 inches   1 cm = 0.39 inches   1 dm = 3.94 inches   1 m = 39.37 inches

0 in.   1 in.   2 in.   3 in.   4 in.

Edible Plant

Ht: 3 dm

MOUNTAIN SORREL

Oxyria digyna / **POLYGONACEAE** Buckwheat family

Other Common Names: Scurvy Grass, Alpine Sorrel

Description: Perennial, alpine herb 1-3 dm (rarely more) high; root, deep, large, fleshy; stems and leaves mostly basal; leaves succulent, round to kidney-shaped, 1 or 2 to a stem; flower stalk, long, narrow, bearing dense clusters of small green-to-red flowers or small, reddish seed capsules.

Range: Higher altitudes of North America; alpine timberline to summits of Cascade and Rocky Mountains; New England Appalachian Mountains and the American Arctic.

Season: Harvested in spring, summer and early fall.

Edible: Leaves and stems.

Preparation: Leaves and stems are harvested at any time, but best before flowers appear. These are eaten raw or cooked. Simmer with fish heads for a fine broth. Leaves can be stored until they ferment slightly, then used as a substitute for sauerkraut.

Notes of Interest: The synonym Scurvy Grass is given because of the high vitamin C content. Plant is commonly known by this name in the Arctic.

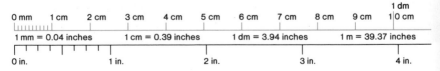

| 0 mm | 1 cm | 2 cm | 3 cm | 4 cm | 5 cm | 6 cm | 7 cm | 8 cm | 9 cm | 1 dm 10 cm |

| 1 mm = 0.04 inches | 1 cm = 0.39 inches | 1 dm = 3.94 inches | 1 m = 39.37 inches |

| 0 in. | 1 in. | 2 in. | 3 in. | 4 in. |

Edible Plant

NETTLE

Urtica dioica / **URTICACEAE** **Nettle family**

Other Common Names: Stinging Nettle.

Description: *Urtica:* Annual or perennial herb 1 dm to 5 m tall, armed with stinging hairs; leaves opposite and sharply toothed; flowers very small in dense, frequently drooping clusters. *Urtica dioica:* Perennial herb 7 dm to 3 m tall; creeping rootstalk; leaves are roughly heart-shaped at base, 4-8 cm broad; stems and leaves covered with stinging hairs; green flowers are in slender drooping spikes at leaf-axils.

Range: Widely distributed throughout the U.S. and Canada; frequently in rich, moist, shaded areas. *Urtica dioica* var. *lyallii*, shown here, is common from Alaska to California east to western Montana.

Season: Early spring until late fall.

Edible: Leaves and young stems.

Preparation: Leaves and young stems are harvested, using perhaps Mullein leaves or leather gloves to protect hands. Rinse the greens lightly and steam them for two or three minutes. The toxin is neutralized both by cooking and drying.

Notes of Interest: Substantially endowed with vitamin C and chlorophyll. The cambium layer of the stems of mature plants can be twisted and braided into extraordinary cord which makes fine fishing line. This plant is a contact poison which causes temporary irritation to exposed skin.

0 mm	1 cm	2 cm	3 cm	4 cm	5 cm	6 cm	7 cm	8 cm	9 cm	1 dm / 10 cm

1 mm = 0.04 inches	1 cm = 0.39 inches	1 dm = 3.94 inches	1 m = 39.37 inches

0 in.	1 in.	2 in.	3 in.	4 in.

Edible Plant

Ht: 7 dm

OAK

Quercus garryana / **FAGACEAE**   **Oak family**

Other Common Names: White Oak, *Q. garryana*: Oregon Oak

Description: *Quercus:* Rough barked, hardwood trees or shrubs 5-25 m high; deciduous or evergreen leaves, simple, alternate, lobes obtuse without bristle tips or acute with bristle tips; fruit, nut (acorn), 1-3 nuts, each borne in a scaly cup. *Q. garryana:* Sturdy tree 7-20 m tall with rounded or fanshaped crown; bark whitish, deeply grooved and checked; leaves, leathery, dark green, shiny above and dull or rust colored underside; leaf lobes, 5-9, obtuse and unbristled; acorn borne in shallow cup.

Range: *Quercus:* Widely distributed throughout most of North America; relatively dry, sterile plains and hillsides.

Season: Supplies edibles in autumn.

Edible: Nut (acorn).

Preparation: Mature nuts usually fall to ground. Shell should be inspected for pinholes, an indication of wormy nut. After washing and tasting for bitterness, nut can be eaten. Nuts unpleasantly bitter are roasted; those very bitter will have to be boiled or soaked in one or more changes of water to remove tannic acid. Nuts then sun dried or made into dough which can be baked into bread or roasted for biscuits.

Notes of Interest: The acorn from the White Oak is generally sweeter and more apt to be palatable raw.

0 mm	1 cm	2 cm	3 cm	4 cm	5 cm	6 cm	7 cm	8 cm	9 cm	1 dm 10 cm

1 mm = 0.04 inches	1 cm = 0.39 inches	1 dm = 3.94 inches	1 m = 39.37 inches

0 in.	1 in.	2 in.	3 in.	4 in.

OREGON GRAPE

Berberis nervosa / **BERBERIDACEAE**   **Barberry family**

Other Common Names: Long-leaved Oregon Grape

Description: *Berberis:* Low, rigid shrub, erect stems, characterized by yellow wood; leaves leathery, prickly evergreen; flowers borne along stem are yellow; fruit, berry, 1 to several. *B. nervosa:* Stems 3-6 dm long, from lengthy rootstalk; compound leaves 9-15, semi-glossy above and prominently veined, spiny-toothed; flowers in elongated terminal clusters, are yellow; berries are dark blue, waxy surface coated with a fine whitish powder.

Range: *Berberis:* Found in coniferous forests in most types of soil from the Rocky Mountains to the Pacific Coast, including British Columbia to approximately 2000 m.

Season: Flowers in the spring; fruit ripens in autumn.

Edible: Primarily the berries.

Preparation: The berry is edible raw, however the taste is improved after the first frost. The pleasantly acid berry is used in jams, jellies, sauces, and wines. In all applications the berry is better and sweeter following an autumn frost.

Notes of Interest: Large quantities of the roots of *Berberis* are shipped yearly to Eastern pharmaceutical houses where they extract the alkaloid drug, berberine, bitter yellow crystals used among other things as a tonic. Roots are also crushed and boiled to produce yellow dye.

0 mm	1 cm	2 cm	3 cm	4 cm	5 cm	6 cm	7 cm	8 cm	9 cm	1 dm 10 cm

1 mm = 0.04 inches	1 cm = 0.39 inches	1 dm = 3.94 inches	1 m = 39.37 inches

0 in.	1 in.	2 in.	3 in.	4 in.

**Edible Plant**

PEPPERGRASS

Lepidium perfoliatum / CRUCIFERAE   Mustard family

Other Common Names: Yellow-flowered Peppergrass

Description: *Lepidium:* Annual or perennial herbs; leaves are undivided to compound, arrow-shaped or with small lobes; flowers small, in elongated terminal clusters; petals white to yellow or absent; pods generally round to oval, flattened. *L. perfoliatum:* Widely branched, 1-4 dm high; basal leaves compound with primary leaflets again compound divided into narrow, linear base, lower stem leaves similar with broad, deeply heart-shaped base, the upper with base alone developed; tiny flowers are yellow; seeds brown, narrow winged. Drawing is of *Lepidium campestre.*

Range: Abundant in open dry and waste places, roadsides, widely spread throughout the northern United States and Canada.

Season: Leaves in spring; seed pods ripen in August.

Edible: Leaves in spring and early summer, and seed pods before ripening.

Preparation: The young leaves are suitable in salad. The primary use of this plant, however, is the use of the seeds as a flavoring for salads, stews, soups and meats.

Notes of Interest: There is a surprising amount of nutritional value in *Lepidium,* including vitamins A, B, C and E. Most species of this plant are native of Europe. *Lepidium* was used as a scurvy preventative in the absence of fresh fruits by seamen.

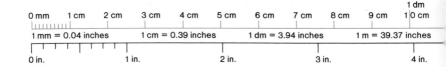

PINE

Pinus contorta / **PINACEAE   Pine family**

Other Common Names: Coast Pine, Black Pine, Lodge-pole Pine

Description: *Pinus:* Evergreen trees or shrubs with small, thin, dry, primary leaves, and secondary green and needle-like, in bundles of 2 to 5, with primary leaves about the base of the bundle; oval cone with woody, shingle-like scales; seeds mostly winged. *P. contorta:* Small, slender to stout tree, depending on environment, to 10 m tall, occasionally more; bark is rough, thick, and dark; leaves in 2s, 3.5-6.5 cm long and sharply pointed; fruiting cones 5-6 cm long, oval; seeds 4 mm long, wing 10-12 mm.

Range: *Pinus:* Found in many locations, depending on species, throughout the United States and Canada from sea level to 3000 meters.

Season: Needles anytime; seeds from maturing cones in autumn.

Edible: Young tender needles and seeds (nuts) from cone.

Preparation: The young needles can be eaten raw. Preferably young, but even mature needles can be used for tea by pouring boiling water over a sufficient quantity of them and steeping to taste. Strain off needles and drink. The pine seeds of some species *(P. contorta* included) are large enough to provide nourishment. Burn cones to roast and loosen seeds. Crush remains to remove seeds.

Notes of Interest: Pine needles are high in vitamin A, and supply 5 times as much vitamin C as an equal amount of lemon. Lodge-pole Pine *(P. latifolia)* was important to Indians of the West for use in framing tepees.

| | | | | | | | | | | 1 dm |
| 0 mm | 1 cm | 2 cm | 3 cm | 4 cm | 5 cm | 6 cm | 7 cm | 8 cm | 9 cm | 10 cm |

| 1 mm = 0.04 inches | 1 cm = 0.39 inches | 1 dm = 3.94 inches | 1 m = 39.37 inches |

| 0 in. | 1 in. | 2 in. | 3 in. | 4 in. |

PLANTAIN

Plantago lanceolata / **PLANTAGINACEAE**   **Plantain family**

Other Common Names: Indian Wheat, *P. lanceolata:* English Plantain

Description: *Plantago:* Annual or perennial herb 2 cm to 8 dm tall; leaves vary from linear to egg-shape; stems bear dense terminal spike of small inconspicuous flowers. *P. lanceolata:* Perennial herb 2-8 dm tall; dense, long soft hairs at base; leaves, edges finely irregular, lancelike, 7-28 cm long, tapering to stalk; dense spike 3-9 cm long, mostly single, brown in color.

Range: *Plantago:* Widely distributed throughout North America; open fields, disturbed ground up to 3100 m.

Season: Appears in the spring; leaves harvested in spring and early summer.

Edible: Primarily leaves.

Preparation: Leaves are best (less fibrous) when young; used as a potherb. Although edible raw, leaves are preferable cooked. More mature leaves are dried and crushed, mixing a handful with two cups of boiling water. Allow brew to steep for thirty minutes, reheat and drink.

Notes of Interest: There are several medicinal applications of this plant. A poultice made from mashed fresh leaves can be applied to insect bites, stings, burns, and other minor wounds. Seeds soaked for several hours and eaten raw act as a laxative.

									1 dm
0 mm	1 cm	2 cm	3 cm	4 cm	5 cm	6 cm	7 cm	8 cm	9 cm	10 cm

1 mm = 0.04 inches   1 cm = 0.39 inches   1 dm = 3.94 inches   1 m = 39.37 inches

0 in.   1 in.   2 in.   3 in.   4 in.

PRAIRIE SMOKE

Geum triflorum / **ROSACEAE Rose family**

Other Common Names: Old Man's Whiskers, Grandfather's Beard

Description: *Geum:* Perennial herbs 3-10 dm high, with creeping underground stems; mostly basal leaves are compound and few reduced stemborne leaves; flowers single or clustered, yellow, pink, purple or white. *G. triflorum:* Softly haired simple flowering stems 20-45 cm high; forking at top, bearing only reduced leaves; basal leaves tufted and compound feather-like with 9-20 lobed and toothed leaflets; flowers nodding, usually 3 on a flower stalk, are purple to yellow with a purple tinge.

Range: *Geum:* Found throughout North America in coniferous forests, dry to moist prairies, rocky hillsides to 2500 m.

Season: Blooms April through June, occasionally into July.

Edible: Roots.

Preparation: The root can be boiled, producing a weak tea-like drink.

Notes of Interest: The species name *triflorum* means 3-flowered. This plant has an unusual seed dispersement in that the seed is carried by the wind on a long feathery style which acts as a sail making for wide distribution of this attractive plant. In old England the roots of *Geum* were allowed to marinate in wine and were consumed to relieve heart trouble.

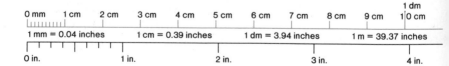

0 mm	1 cm	2 cm	3 cm	4 cm	5 cm	6 cm	7 cm	8 cm	9 cm	1 dm 10 cm

1 mm = 0.04 inches   1 cm = 0.39 inches   1 dm = 3.94 inches   1 m = 39.37 inches

0 in.	1 in.	2 in.	3 in.	4 in.

Edible Plant

Ht: 7 dm

PRICKLY PEAR CACTUS

Opuntia polyacantha / **CACTACEAE Cactus family**

Other Common Names: Indian Figs, Many-spined Prickly Pear, Beavertail

Description: *Opuntia:* Stem jointed, branched, fleshy, succulent, spiny perennials lacking well-defined green foliage; leaves primarily in the form of spines or dry scales, tipped with numerous fine barbs and woolly hairs; flowers are in the shape of a cup. *O. polyacantha:* Stems prostrate, forming compressed pear-shaped pads 5-11 cm long; solitary flowers are yellow and without stalk.

Range: *Opuntia:* Found in desert areas throughout the West and Southwest as far north as the Peace River region of west central Canada and as far south as Baja.

Season: Blooms from March through June depending on the latitude.

Edible: Primarily the pulp of both pads and stems, and the fruit.

Preparation: The fleshy joints connecting the spiny pads can be roasted, boiled, stewed or fried, but the spines should be removed first, either by burning or slicing. The pads can be split lengthwise and the fleshy pulp scooped out. The fruit of the larger species is excellent

Notes of Interest: Early Spanish explorers of the new world returned home with *Opuntia* introducing it to Europe where it has now spread to most of the warmer countries.

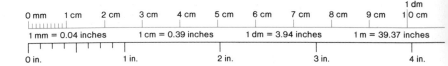

0 mm	1 cm	2 cm	3 cm	4 cm	5 cm	6 cm	7 cm	8 cm	9 cm	1 dm 10 cm

1 mm = 0.04 inches   1 cm = 0.39 inches   1 dm = 3.94 inches   1 m = 39.37 inches

0 in.	1 in.	2 in.	3 in.	4 in.

Edible Plant

Ht: 10 cm

Opuntia polyacantha **Cactus Family**

Opuntia polyacantha / 163

PURSLANE

Portulaca oleracea / **PORTULACACEAE**   **Purslane family**

Other Common Names: None

Description: Succulent, annual herb; basal branching stems 5-30 cm long; ascending or prone; leaves alternate, widest at tip, tapering gradually or abruptly to the base; small, stalkless, yellow flowers bloom in little terminal clusters at stem branching points.

Range: Widely distributed throughout North America in low to moderate elevations; common to cultivated areas or otherwise disturbed ground.

Season: Spring until first frost; blooms in mid summer.

Edible: Primarily leaves and branches.

Preparation: Young, tender leaves and branches picked from the plant top are edible raw or cooked. This tart, crisp green makes an excellent salad. Used in soup it adds flavor and body. Larger young stems can be cut and pickled. The entire above ground plant is edible, but should be rinsed first to remove some of the gritty texture.

Notes of Interest: In many countries, including the United States (Southwest) this plant is commercially harvested. Among the most commonly harvested plant and vegetable greens, only Parsley exceeds Purslane in iron content; surprisingly, because Purslane is approximately 93% water.

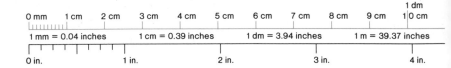

Edible Plant

Ht: 9 cm

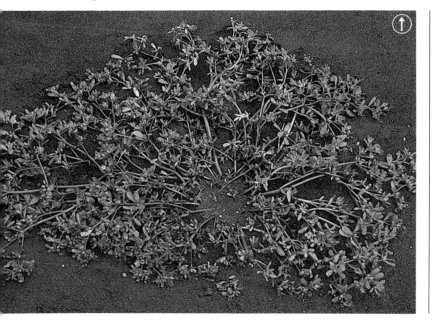

REED GRASS

Phragmites communis / **GRAMINEAE**   **Grass family**

Other Common Names: Reed, Common Reed, Carrizo

Description: Very tall, perennial, marsh grass 2-4 m high; stems stout, jointed, hollow or pithy, rise from long creeping rootstalk; leaves broad, 1.5-5 cm wide; flowers in terminal clusters 1.5-4 dm long, diffusely branched, roughly elongated pyramidal, covered with long silky hairs.

Range: Widely distributed throughout North America; swamps and marshes.

Season: Harvested whenever identified.

Edible: Rootstalks, young shoots and leaves, seeds.

Preparation: Washed rootstalks are eaten raw, roasted or boiled. Young shoots and leaves serve as a potherb, and the seeds, collected in autumn, can be boiled in their hulls or dried and ground.

Notes of Interest: Mexicans and Indians of the southwestern United States used this plant in numerous applications. The reed was used for arrow shafts and weaving rods. The stems and leaves made suitable weaving material, the fibers of the plant were twisted together for cordage which found its way into fishing nets, mats, etc. This plant was also used for thatching.

0 mm	1 cm	2 cm	3 cm	4 cm	5 cm	6 cm	7 cm	8 cm	9 cm	1 dm 10 cm

1 mm = 0.04 inches   1 cm = 0.39 inches   1 dm = 3.94 inches   1 m = 39.37 inches

0 in.   1 in.   2 in.   3 in.   4 in.

Edible Plant

Ht: 2.5 m

SALAL

Gaultheria shallon / **ERICACEAE**   **Heath family**

Other Common Names: Common Salal

Description: *Gaultheria:* Low trailing, erect or prostrate evergreen shrub; evergreen leaves, shiny, clustered near tip of erect branches; flowers solitary or in elongated, unbranched cluster, white or pinkish. *G. shallon:* Rigid freely branching shrub, 5-30 dm or more high; leaves are oblong-egg-shaped and finely toothed, alternate, leathery, dark green and shiny on top, pale beneath; flower clusters are terminal, 5-15 flowered, white or pinkish; fruit spherical, powdery, purple nearly black appearing 7-10 mm in diameter.

Range: Widely spread throughout the United States and Canada, most frequent in coastal regions of the East and West in thickets and woods to 1500 m.

Season: Berries available in August and September.

Edible: Fruit (berry).

Preparation: There are numerous ways to use this berry as food, such as jams, jellies, pies, syrup or mashed and dried for winter use, as was done by coastal Indians (particularly of the Northwest Pacific coast).

Notes of Interest: Salal was the name given *Gaultheria shallon* by the coastal Indians of Oregon. Captain Meriwether Lewis of the Lewis and Clark expedition collected the fruit of this plant at the mouth of the Columbia River.

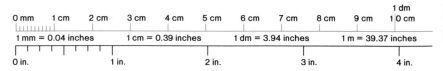

Edible Plant

Ht: 22 dm

SERVICEBERRY

Amelanchier alnifolia / **ROSACEAE**   **Rose family**

Other Common Names: Juneberry, Shadberry, Saskatoon

Description: *Amelanchier:* Deciduous, branching shrub or small tree up to 10 m high; leaves simple, alternate; flowers, white, clustered, borne along stem on individual stalks of equal length or in flat-topped cluster. *A. alnifolia:* Shrub .5-10 m high; leaves round or round-oblong, coarsely toothed upper half, rounded at ends, thinly hairy above, frequently densely hairy below; flowers borne along stem; berries purple to black 10-15 mm in diameter.

Range: *Amelanchier:* Widely distributed throughout North America to 2300 m; moist to somewhat dry ground, in open woods, clearings or by lakes and streams.

Season: Blossoms in spring; provides edibles from early summer through fall; fruit begins to dry on the vine (still edible) in late summer and is available into winter.

Edible: Fruit (berry).

Preparation: Generally sweet and pulpy berries are eaten raw or cooked, or mashed and dried for storage. Preserves and pies made with this berry are superb. The flavor of muffins, griddlecakes and other baked items is enhanced with its generous use. Wine is also made from the Serviceberry.

Notes of Interest: Like the Currant, this berry was used by the Indians as an ingredient for making pemmican.

0 mm	1 cm	2 cm	3 cm	4 cm	5 cm	6 cm	7 cm	8 cm	9 cm	1 dm 10 cm

1 mm = 0.04 inches	1 cm = 0.39 inches	1 dm = 3.94 inches	1 m = 39.37 inches

0 in.	1 in.	2 in.	3 in.	4 in.

Edible Plant

Ht: 12 dm

SHEEP SORREL

Rumex acetosella / **POLYGONACEAE Buckwheat family**

Other Common Names: *R. acetosella:* Rose Sorrel

Description: *Rumex:* Mostly perennial (some annual) coarse herb 1 dm to 2.5 m tall; basal leaves generally large, alternate, grooved, stemmed; flowers green, occasionally red or yellow; frequently borne in circular array in loose terminal clusters. *R. acetosella:* Perennial herb 1-6 dm tall; stems slender, generally clustered from long, slender, creeping rootstalks; lower leaves oblong, mostly arrow-shaped with 2 lobes at base; upper leaves lance-like, small, lobeless; flowers mostly red.

Range: *Rumex:* Widely distributed throughout much of North America; fields, cultivated ground and piedmont valleys.

Season: Primarily used as edible in spring and early summer.

Edible: Leaves.

Preparation: Young leaves are tart but pleasant tasting raw. Leaves used as substitute for vinegar, lemon, and lime in a variety of ways including seasoning fish by baking or frying with leaves placed inside. Soups and salads are deliciously flavored with these leaves.

Notes of Interest: Sheep Sorrel is a native of Europe and European cookbooks frequently contain recipes utilizing the leaves of this plant. Plant is an abundant source of vitamin C.

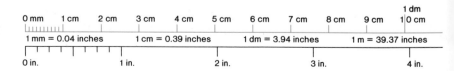

0 mm	1 cm	2 cm	3 cm	4 cm	5 cm	6 cm	7 cm	8 cm	9 cm	1 dm 10 cm

1 mm = 0.04 inches   1 cm = 0.39 inches   1 dm = 3.94 inches   1 m = 39.37 inches

| 0 in. | | 1 in. | | 2 in. | | 3 in. | | 4 in. |

Edible Plant

Ht: 3dm

SHEPHERD'S PURSE

Capsella bursa-pastoris / **CRUCIFERAE** **Mustard family**

Other Common Names: None

Description: Branching, annual herb, 1-5 dm tall; stem slightly hairy arising from a rosette of tufted, gradually tapering or oblong, toothed or deeply cleft, basal leaves; upper leaves small, not cleft; multiple stalks support long, terminal clusters of small white flowers which have 4 petals; heart-shaped seed pods stand erect from short stalks, broad ends up.

Range: Widely distributed throughout North America; dry open cultivated and waste ground; common in gardens and fields.

Season: Spring, summer and fall.

Edible: Leaves, roots and seeds.

Preparation: Spring leaves are eaten raw or blanched and used in salads. Older leaves are tough and require boiling. The seeds should be roasted and ground before mixing with flour or mush. Roots can be dried and ground to be used in stews, soups, etc., for a flavoring similar to ginger.

Notes of Interest: This plant is named for purse-shaped seed pods along its multiple stems. Shepherd's Purse is an abundant source of vitamins A and C. Vitamin K, the blood clotting vitamin, is also available from this plant.

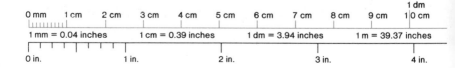

| 0 mm | 1 cm | 2 cm | 3 cm | 4 cm | 5 cm | 6 cm | 7 cm | 8 cm | 9 cm | 1 dm 10 cm |

1 mm = 0.04 inches   1 cm = 0.39 inches   1 dm = 3.94 inches   1 m = 39.37 inches

| 0 in. | 1 in. | 2 in. | 3 in. | 4 in. |

Edible Plant

Ht: 4 dm

SHOOTING STAR

Dodecatheon hendersonii / **PRIMULACEAE** **Primrose family**

Other Common Names: Henderson Shooting Star, Broad-leaved Shooting Star

Description: *Dodecatheon:* Perennial herbs with leafless flower stalk, either hairless or with light glandular hairs; leaves basal, either smooth-edged or toothed; single flower stalk bears a showy terminal flower cluster, white to purple. *D. hendersonii:* Plant hairless with stout, short base, with fleshy but fibrous roots; leaves circular to egg-shape, 2.5-7 cm long, rapidly narrowing to leafstalk; flowering stem 1-4 dm high with a 3-10 flowered head, rose to purple with a blackish basal zone.

Range: *Dodecatheon:* Mostly moist or wet ground. *D. hendersonii,* from New Mexico to Saskatchewan, Canada; found in generally dry open woods and occasional hillsides, from about 800-2800 meters.

Season: Blooms March and April.

Edible: Roots and leaves.

Preparation: The roots can be baked, boiled or roasted. The leaves are best boiled or roasted.

Notes of Interest: The genus name, *Dodecatheon,* is from the Greek *dodeca,* twelve, and *Theos,* god. It was believed that this plant was under the care of the twelve superior gods.

										1 dm
0 mm	1 cm	2 cm	3 cm	4 cm	5 cm	6 cm	7 cm	8 cm	9 cm	10 cm

1 mm = 0.04 inches   1 cm = 0.39 inches   1 dm = 3.94 inches   1 m = 39.37 inches

| 0 in. | | 1 in. | | 2 in. | | 3 in. | | 4 in. |

SILVERWEED

Potentilla anserina / **ROSACEAE** **Rose family**

Other Common Names: Cinquefoil

Description: *Potentilla:* Annual, perennial or biennial herbs or shrubs .5-12 dm high; leaves mostly compound; flowers borne singly or clustered; petals mostly yellow, sometimes red or white. *P. anserina:* Low, perennial herb with rooting basal branches; leaves and flower-stems closely clustered at root-top; compound leaves 1-3 dm long; leaflets, 11-13, feather-like, toothed, shiny green above and silvery-white beneath; flowers yellow, borne singly. Drawing is *P. pacifica,* nearly identical to, but slightly larger than *P. anserina.*

Range: *Potentilla:* Distributed across much of Canada and northern United States, and along the West Coast and Rocky Mountains; found in both damp and very dry ground; prefers alkaline soil, marshes, moist meadows, and coastal areas.

Season: Blooms in spring and early summer depending upon location; edible in spring and fall.

Edible: Root is harvested in spring and late fall.

Preparation: Large, fleshy root is edible raw, roasted or boiled and mashed or fried. Root is also dried for storage.

Notes of Interest: This plant was used, where available, extensively in the Indian diet and was so prized that roots might be given as a wedding gift.

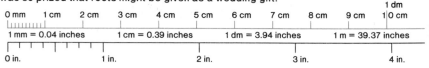

0 mm	1 cm	2 cm	3 cm	4 cm	5 cm	6 cm	7 cm	8 cm	9 cm	1 dm 10 cm

1 mm = 0.04 inches   1 cm = 0.39 inches   1 dm = 3.94 inches   1 m = 39.37 inches

0 in.	1 in.	2 in.	3 in.	4 in.

Edible Plant

Ht: 1.5 dm

SPEEDWELL

Veronica americana / **SCROPHULARIACEAE** **Figwort family**

Other Common Names: Brooklime, Water Speedwell, *V. americana:* Common Speedwell

Description: *Veronica:* Perennial or annual shrubs or herbs (mostly herbs) to 10 dm tall; leaves all or partly opposite; flowers solitary or clustered along stem. *V. americana:* Perennial herb 2-6 dm tall; stems, succulent, smooth, trailing or ascending, rooting at stem joints; leaves oblong egg-shaped to lance-like, toothed; blue flowers, small, lobed in 4s, loosely clustered, from stem-leaf juncture.

Range: *Veronica:* Eastern and western areas of North America including the Rocky Mountains; along streams, moist and wet places. Several species including *V. alpina,* found up to 4000 meters.

Season: Blooms late spring to early summer.

Edible: Leaves and stems.

Preparation: Upper plant leaves and stems, harvested before flower appears, can be eaten raw or used in salads. After flowering these parts are better boiled to eliminate the somewhat bitter taste. Also used as a potherb.

Notes of Interest: Speedwell was once used extensively, when fruit was unavailable, as a scurvy preventative. The plant is high in vitamin C.

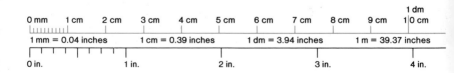

| 0 mm | 1 cm | 2 cm | 3 cm | 4 cm | 5 cm | 6 cm | 7 cm | 8 cm | 9 cm | 1 dm 10 cm |

1 mm = 0.04 inches   1 cm = 0.39 inches   1 dm = 3.94 inches   1 m = 39.37 inches

| 0 in. | 1 in. | 2 in. | 3 in. | 4 in. |

Veronica americana / 181

SPRING BEAUTY

Claytonia lanceolata / **PORTULACACEAE** **Purslane family**

Other Common Names: Narrow Leaved Spring Beauty, Fairy Spuds

Description: *Claytonia:* Succulent perennial herb from a deep corm or fleshy root; simple opposite, alternate or basal stem leaves; flowers are above stem leaves, mostly distributed along an axis, 2 to 6 petals, irregular, mostly pinkish. *C. lanceolata:* Stems 3-8 cm high from a spherical tuber 1-2 cm in diameter; basal leaves none to few, are lance-like 3-5 cm long, leaves borne on stem above base are not united, lance-like to narrowly oval, 2-7 cm long; flowers along stem few to many are white or pink with reddish lines.

Range: *Claytonia:* Sunny stream banks and rich, moist open woods from Alaska to Nova Scotia and south to Texas. *C. lanceolata:* Found in rich subalpine woods and meadows, frequently near melting snow banks, 1700 to 2350 m.

Season: Blooms with retreating snow in late April and May into the summer.

Edible: Tuber, leaves, flowers.

Preparation: The small fleshy tuber is excellent raw, boiled or roasted. Boil tuber for abou 12 minutes in salted water. Remove the skin (if you prefer) and eat, or add to salads and stews. The young leaves and flowers can be used in salads.

Notes of Interest: Although there are more than 50 species of *Claytonia* throughout the world, *C. lanceolata* is not always found in abundance and therefore careful note should be made of its local status before harvesting.

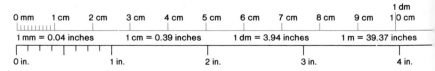

Edible Plant

Ht: 3 cm

Claytonia lanceolata **Purslane Family**

Claytonia lanceolata / 183

STONECROP

Sedum lanceolatum / **CRASSULACEAE** **Stonecrop family**

Other Common Names: Roseroot, Orpine, *S. lanceolatum* and *S. stenopetalum:* Yellow Stonecrop

Description: *Sedum:* Perennial or biennial, mostly mat-like herb .5-4 dm high; stems low, leafy, leaves fleshy, flat to cylindric; terminal flowers appear first; flower color white, yellow or red. *S. lanceolatum:* Perennial herb with erect stems 5-20 cm tall; branches spreading from rootstalk are very leafy and form spongy-like basal rosettes; leaves lance-like to somewhat cylindric; yellow flowers are star-like. The drawing is of *S. rhodanthum* which has rose or sometimes white colored flowers.

Range: Widely distributed over North America (except for Southern area); sea level to mountains, rocky ground, cliff bottoms and ledges, in moist soil.

Season: Blooms in early summer; edible early spring to late fall.

Edible: Leaves, stems and rootstalk.

Preparation: Early leaves and stems are edible raw or used in salads. Later, until plant blooms, the harvested portions should be cooked until tender or used as potherb. Root stalks are boiled. Rootstalks should also be harvested before plant blooms or in fall when new growth and fresh, crisp rootstalks appear.

Notes of Interest: The fleshy leaves store much moisture; however, it is used during dry summer months rendering the plant less than palatable.

0 mm	1 cm	2 cm	3 cm	4 cm	5 cm	6 cm	7 cm	8 cm	9 cm	1 dm 10 cm

1 mm = 0.04 inches   1 cm = 0.39 inches   1 dm = 3.94 inches   1 m = 39.37 inches

0 in.	1 in.	2 in.	3 in.	4 in.

Edible Plant

Ht: 9 cm

SUNFLOWER

Helianthus annuus / **COMPOSITAE**   **Sunflower family**

Other Common Names: Common Sunflower, *H. annuus:* Kansas Sunflower

Description: *Helianthus:* Coarse annual or perennial herb 3 dm to 3 m tall; leaves simple, opposite, rough, toothed; large, conspicuous, yellow, ray-like flowers surround red-purple or brown disk-shaped flowers; produces numerous seeds. *.H. annuus:* Erect, stout stemmed, annual herb, 3-20 dm tall; stalk fibrous and prickly hairy; leaves triangular to diamond-egg-shaped; flower up to 15 cm diameter; seed head purplish brown. Drawing is of *H. pumilus,* a perennial.

Range: *Helianthus:* Widely distributed throughout North America; plains, open fields, open woods, and grassy slopes.

Season: Blossoms in April or May, lasts into fall; seeds mature in fall.

Edible: Seeds, roots of some species.

Preparation: Seed head is cut off and seed rubbed or ground out. Seeds parched and eaten, hull and all, or hulled and ground. Hulled seeds are heated (n cooked) for mush. Dark-roasted seed shells can be ground and brewed as coffee. Roo (of edible species, i.e., *H. maximiliannii, H. nuttallii*) are roasted or boiled.

Notes of Interest: Sunflower seeds contain extraordinary nourishment. 100 grams of see contains 360 calories; seeds are 52% crude protein and 27% carbohydrate.

0 mm	1 cm	2 cm	3 cm	4 cm	5 cm	6 cm	7 cm	8 cm	9 cm	1 dm 10 cm

1 mm = 0.04 inches   1 cm = 0.39 inches   1 dm = 3.94 inches   1 m = 39.37 inches

0 in.   1 in.   2 in.   3 in.   4 in.

Ht: 2 m

THISTLE

Cirsium arvense / **COMPOSITAE** **Sunflower family**

Other Common Names: *C. arvense:* Canada Thistle

Description: *Cirsium:* Stout, spiny, biennial or perennial herb 1-20 dm tall; leaves alternate, toothed or deeply cleft, spined-edges; white to pink to purple flower head is disk-like, single or few at ends of branches; lower half of flower head bristly. *C. arvense:* Perennial herb 4-12 dm tall; branches ascend from deep, creeping roots; leaves lance-like prickly, 1-2 dm long; flowers purple.

Range: *Cirsium:* Throughout much of North America; meadows, clearings, wooded areas and dry waste places.

Season: Blooms spring and early summer; edibles spring and summer.

Edible: Roots, stems and seeds.

Preparation: Roots eaten raw, boiled or roasted, as can the peeled stems. Young peeled stems yield prime food. Cut the spiked leaves from the stalk before harvesting either stem or root. Boiled, the peeled stem has a cooked celery flavor consistency. Seeds are eaten raw or roasted.

Notes of Interest: The dry, fluffy seed material makes excellent tinder. Truman Everts, an early explorer (1870) of Yellowstone National Park was saved from starvation while lost for a time in the park by eating *C. foliosum*.

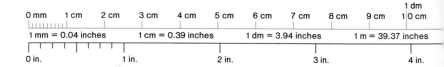

| 0 mm | 1 cm | 2 cm | 3 cm | 4 cm | 5 cm | 6 cm | 7 cm | 8 cm | 9 cm | 1 dm 10 cm |

1 mm = 0.04 inches   1 cm = 0.39 inches   1 dm = 3.94 inches   1 m = 39.37 inches

0 in.   1 in.   2 in.   3 in.   4 in.

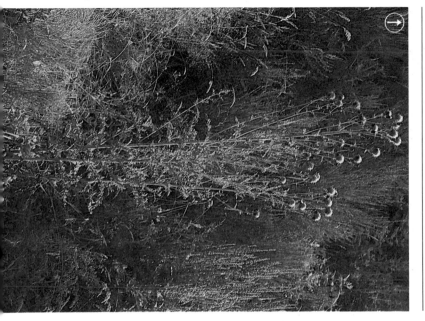

WAPPATO

Sagittaria latifolia / **ALISMACEAE** **Water Plaintain family**

Other Common Names: Arrowhead, Duckpotato, *S. latifolia:* Broad-leafed Arrowhead

Description: *Sagittaria:* Perennial aquatic or marsh herb 3-8 dm tall; fleshy rootstalks; long basal leafstalk with terminal arrow-shaped leaves; conspicuous waxy, white flowers borne in 3s near end of stem. S. latifolia: Flowering stalks, mostly unbranched 2-7 dm tall; leaf blade broad, basal lobes widely spreading.

Range: *Sagittaria:* Throughout North America; wet ground, shallow water, marshes, ponds, edges of lakes, or very slow streams, moderate altitudes.

Season: Long-lived flowers bloom in mid-summer; root tubers harvested in fall.

Edible: Tubers.

Preparation: Smooth, starchy tubers are harvested by wading, feeling with hands and pulling or grubbing in mud with feet and toes (Indian method). The tubers, located along underground runners, may be several feet from plant. When dislodged, they float to surface. Tubers are best roasted or boiled. Boiled tubers can be sliced, dried and stored for later use.

Notes of Interest: During their stay on the lower Columbia River, the Lewis and Clark expedition used this plant extensively in their diet.

1 dm

0 mm	1 cm	2 cm	3 cm	4 cm	5 cm	6 cm	7 cm	8 cm	9 cm	10 cm

1 mm = 0.04 inches   1 cm = 0.39 inches   1 dm = 3.94 inches   1 m = 39.37 inches

0 in.	1 in.	2 in.	3 in.	4 in.

Edible Plant

Ht: 4.5 dm

WATERCRESS

Rorippa nasturtium-aquaticum / **CRUCIFERAE**   **Mustard family**

Other Common Names: None

Description: *Rorippa:* Branching annual or perennial herb; leaves, mostly smooth, toothed, lobed or divided; slender, cylindrical seed pods; flowers tiny to medium are white or yellow. *R. nasturtium-aquaticum:* Succulent aquatic perennial herb with creeping stems 1-7 dm long, erect or prostrate; lower leaves simple, those above oblong or egg-shaped leaflets, 3-7, terminal leaflet being largest; small white flowers borne along stem in terminal clusters.

Range: *Rorippa:* Throughout North America; submerged or partly submerged in slow moving streams, springs and in marshes.

Season: Spring, summer and fall.

Edible: Primarily leaves.

Preparation: Harvest only portions which grow above water; submerged parts, including roots, should be considered unpalatable. This plant is excellent raw or used in salads, and like many non-aquatic greens, makes a fine potherb. It has the distinctive taste of pepper and when mixed with bland or mild greens perks up the flavor. Leaves are also steeped for tea.

Notes of Interest: The reputation of this plant is well known throughout the world, not only as an edible, but medicinally as well. The plant is rich in vitamins A, C and E and additionally, contains fair amounts of iron and calcium.

0 mm	1 cm	2 cm	3 cm	4 cm	5 cm	6 cm	7 cm	8 cm	9 cm	1 dm
										10 cm

1 mm = 0.04 inches   1 cm = 0.39 inches   1 dm = 3.94 inches   1 m = 39.37 inches

0 in.   1 in.   2 in.   3 in.   4 in.

WATERLEAF

Hydrophyllum occidentale / **HYDROPHYLLACEAE**   **Waterleaf family**

Other Common Names: None

Description: *Hydrophyllum:* Succulent perennial herbs with horizontal, fleshy, rootstalk; stems and foliage succulent; leaves basal, alternate, cleft or feather-like divided; flower head in loose to dense clusters, blue, lavender or white. *H. occidentale:* Erect, branching plant 2-4 dm tall; hairy solitary stems, pale green; leaves 1-2.5 dm long, 5-7 leaves, mostly 3-parted, coarsely toothed, hairy on both sides; flowers loose, open bell-shaped, bluish or lavender.

Range: *Hydrophyllum:* Found throughout the United States and Canada, in rich damp woods, shaded stream banks and wet meadows to 2500 m.

Season: Flowers May through July depending on region and genus. Provides edibles whenever identified.

Edible: Young shoots, leaves and root.

Preparation: The young shoots and greens are good in salads. The leaves can be used as a lettuce substitute in sandwiches. The rootstalks are great in stew or boiled like carrots but may also be baked or fried.

Notes of Interest: This plant contains vitamins A, C and E and also some iron and calcium.

0 mm 1 cm 2 cm	3 cm 4 cm	5 cm 6 cm 7 cm	8 cm 9 cm	1 dm 10 cm
1 mm = 0.04 inches	1 cm = 0.39 inches	1 dm = 3.94 inches	1 m = 39.37 inches	

0 in.	1 in.	2 in.	3 in. 4 in.

Edible Plant

Ht: 3 dm

WATER SHIELD

Brasenia schreberi / **NYMPHAEACEAE**   **Water-lily family**

Other Common Names: Water-target

Description: Aquatic plant with long slender, branching, underwater stems 3-15 dm long, arising from creeping rootstalks; leafstalk and leaves, except leaf upper surface, slime covered; floating leaves elliptical or oval 5-15 cm in diameter, green above, purplish beneath, stalk attachment to underside near center; purple flowers approximately 16 mm long are inconspicuous.

Range: Widely distributed throughout most of temperate North America; ponds, ditches, sloughs, edges of slow streams.

Season: Provides edibles nearly year-round.

Edible: Thickened rootstalks, young leaf and leafstalk.

Preparation: Tubers can be gathered in much the same way as those of Wappato *(Sagittaria)*. Starchy thickened rootstalks are first peeled then boiled for eating. Rootstalk is also dried to store or to be ground into flour. Young, partially opened leaf and stem is a fair salad ingredient.

Notes of Interest: *B. schreberi* is a native and common in much of the world including Asia, Australia and Africa, in addition to North America.

										1 dm
0 mm	1 cm	2 cm	3 cm	4 cm	5 cm	6 cm	7 cm	8 cm	9 cm	1 0 cm

1 mm = 0.04 inches   1 cm = 0.39 inches   1 dm = 3.94 inches   1 m = 39.37 inches

0 in.   1 in.   2 in.   3 in.   4 in.

Dia: 5-10 cm

WILD CRANBERRY

Vaccinium oxycoccus / **ERICACEAE** **Heath family**

Other Common Names: Small Cranberry, Lowbush Cranberry

Description: *Vaccinium:* Small vine-like to large, sturdy, evergreen or deciduous, erect or depressed shrubs 5 cm to 3 m tall; leaves simple and alternate. *V. oxycoccus:* Vines slender, trailing; short, ascending branches; leaves small, ovate-oblong 10-14 mm long, leathery, smooth but curled edges, whitish undersurface; flowers 2-10 on slender stalk; ends are pink or purple; fruit, a dark red berry 7-9 mm in diameter.

Range: *Vaccinium:* Northern United States and California, Canada and Alaska; in a variety of habitats from bogs to dry mountain slopes, depending upon species.

Season: Blooming period, May and June; fruit ripens in July to September.

Edible: Berry.

Preparation: Most berries are succulent, excellent raw, but also good cooked or dried. These delicious berries make fine preserves and are good in baked items. A refreshing cold drink is made by diluting berry juice with water. Hot drinks are best made from the dried berry.

Notes of Interest: Wild Cranberry fruit is a source of vitamin A, B[1] and C with traces of calcium, phosphorous and iron.

0 mm	1 cm	2 cm	3 cm	4 cm	5 cm	6 cm	7 cm	8 cm	9 cm	1 dm 10 cm

1 mm = 0.04 inches   1 cm = 0.39 inches   1 dm = 3.94 inches   1 m = 39.37 inches

0 in.	1 in.	2 in.	3 in.	4 in.

WILD GRAPE

Vitis californica / **VITACEAE** **Grape family**

Other Common Names: Canyon Grape, *V. californica:* Western Wild Grape

Description: *Vitis:* Woody, climbing vines 2-20 m long, supported by tendrils (coils which cling); large, single axis leaves are conspicuously veined, veins radiating from the base; clustered flowers are opposite leaves. *V. californica:* Purple fruit is dull, coated with fine powdery material; fruit (grape) is juicy and succulent when ripe.

Range: *Vitis:* Found throughout a number of locations in temperate North America; growing in fertile soil along streams, beaches and on the edges of wooded areas.

Season: Edible parts nearly all year; grapes mature in late summer and autumn.

Edible: Fruit, tender shoots and leaves.

Preparation: In spring young shoots and vine tips are eaten raw or steamed. Leaves are steamed as greens. Grapes are eaten raw, cooked, juiced or dried. Fruit makes excellent preserves.

Notes of Interest: Wild Grape leaves can be used to wrap other food for steaming or baking. Wild Grape is exactly like its domestic counterpart, only the berry is smaller.

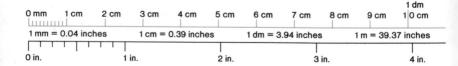

0 mm	1 cm	2 cm	3 cm	4 cm	5 cm	6 cm	7 cm	8 cm	9 cm	1 dm 1 0 cm

1 mm = 0.04 inches   1 cm = 0.39 inches   1 dm = 3.94 inches   1 m = 39.37 inches

0 in.   1 in.   2 in.   3 in.   4 in.

WILD HYACINTH

Brodiaea pulchella / **LILIACEAE** **Lily family**

Other Common Names: Ookow

Description: *Brodiaea:* Perennial herb with flowering stalk 2-10 dm tall; few slender, basal leaves rise from flat-bottomed bulb-like base; flowers in umbrella-like cluster. *B. pulchella:* Flower stalk 4-10 dm tall; 2 or 3 leaves, grass-like, 3-7 dm long, often shriveled when flower appears; flower cluster blue to deep purple.

Range: *Brodiaea:* Western North America in fields and hillsides; some species prefer moist soil.

Season: Blooms in May and early June.

Edible: Bulb-like fleshy stem base.

Preparation: This bulb-like part is eaten raw, roasted, boiled, mashed or dried. It is also excellent when cooked buried in a rock oven with wild game. This slow baking actually seems to sweeten the taste.

Notes of Interest: While plant is in bloom, it is easily distinguished from the Death Camas (*Zigadenus*), and thus is most safely harvested then. This plant is not abundant. (See *About Edible Plants,* page 60.)

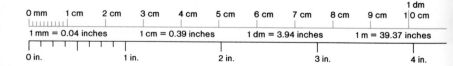

0 mm	1 cm	2 cm	3 cm	4 cm	5 cm	6 cm	7 cm	8 cm	9 cm	1 dm 10 cm

1 mm = 0.04 inches	1 cm = 0.39 inches	1 dm = 3.94 inches	1 m = 39.37 inches

0 in.	1 in.	2 in.	3 in.	4 in.

WILD MUSTARD

Brassica campestris / **CRUCIFERAE**   **Mustard family**

Other Common Names: Common Mustard, Yellow Mustard

Description: *Brassica:* Large, coarse annual or biennial herbs with erect, branching stems 3-10 dm tall; basal leaves stemmed, finely toothed and deeply lobed; upper leaves mostly lobeless are smaller; flowers are yellow, 4-petaled, many, in terminal clusters; *B. campestris:* Coated with a fine powder and nearly hairless; lower leaves sparingly toothed or compound-cleft along leafstalk; flowers in elongated terminal clusters with individual flower stalk slightly woolly-haired, gradually narrowing into a slender beak.

Range: *Brassica:* Found throughout much of North America in open fields, waste ground; frequently a problem weed in cultivated fields.

Season: Found in bloom from April through October.

Edible: Leaves and buds.

Preparation: The leaves are best harvested in spring and should be cooked just below a boil for 30 minutes or more. This green is bitter tasting and is best used to give flavor to bland greens, although it is good cooked with fish or meat. The flower buds are boiled in salted water for 3 to 5 minutes, drained and served with a sprinkling of vinegar.

Notes of Interest: Mustard is a vitamin rich source of A, B^1, B^2 and C in addition to minerals and protein.

0 mm	1 cm	2 cm	3 cm	4 cm	5 cm	6 cm	7 cm	8 cm	9 cm	1 dm 10 cm

1 mm = 0.04 inches   1 cm = 0.39 inches   1 dm = 3.94 inches   1 m = 39.37 inches

0 in.	1 in.	2 in.	3 in.	4 in.

Edible Plant

Ht: 8 dm

WILD ONION

Allium acuminatum / **LILIACEAE** **Lily family**

Other Common Names: Prairie Onion

Description: *Allium:* Perennial herb up to 8 dm tall from bulb; leaves, few, mostly basal, hollow, cylindric or flat, mostly slender; white to purple flowers borne in a terminal umbrella-like or spherical cluster; leaves, stalk and bulb have typical onion or garlic odor and taste. *A. acuminatum:* Stem shoots stout, 1-2.5 dm tall; bulb egg-shaped; leaves, 2-3, narrow, shorter than flowering head; flowers, spherical clusters, 8-30, are pink to bright-rose.

Range: *Allium:* Widely distributed in North America; foothills, high plains, open woods, stony slopes, clay soils up to 3000 m.

Season: Blooms from May to late July depending upon elevation.

Edible: Entire plant.

Preparation: Wild onion is eaten raw or prepared in numerous ways. Nearly any cooking method used to prepare domestic onions is compatible to all wild species including boiling, frying, steaming, creaming for soups, seasoning in stews, etc. Finely chopped leaves are good in salads and stews. The bulb can be stored.

Notes of Interest: Death Camas (*Zygadenus*), a poisonous plant, is similar in appearance; however, it is easily differentiated in that it lacks the onion odor.

0 mm	1 cm	2 cm	3 cm	4 cm	5 cm	6 cm	7 cm	8 cm	9 cm	1 dm 10 cm

1 mm = 0.04 inches   1 cm = 0.39 inches   1 dm = 3.94 inches   1 m = 39.37 inches

0 in.	1 in.	2 in.	3 in.	4 in.

WILD ROSE

Rosa canina / **ROSACEAE** **Rose family**

Other Common Names: Rose Hips, Dog Rose

Description: *Rosa:* Prickly shrubs 1-3 m tall, with compound leaves; leaflets are single connecting opposing pairs; flowers large, showy, solitary or in clusters, pink to deep rose, white or yellow; fruit consists of a small, hard, dry seed enclosed in a fleshy reddish berry-like tube. *R. canina:* Prickles, hooked 3-8 mm long; leaflets are without glands and nearly smooth, sharply toothed edges; flowers are white or pink, 4-4.5 cm broad; fruit scarlet.

Range: Widely distributed throughout the United States and Canada in a wide variety of habitats including thickets, open fields, open woods, ditches and near the seashore from sea level to 2400 m.

Season: Blossoming time varies from May to July, however the fruit (hips) are normally ripe in the fall.

Edible: Rose hips, flowers, leaves.

Preparation: Space will not permit mentioning the many ways to prepare the rose hips. The seeds must be removed before using the fleshy rinds. Although they may be eaten raw they are frequently used in jam, jelly, marmalade, syrup or can be dried or frozen. The flower petals can be eaten raw in a salad. Dried petals and leaves may be used as a tea substitute.

Notes of Interest: Rose hips contain an extremely high amount of vitamin C, with a single fruit yielding up to 10 mg of that vitamin. It is also a source of vitamin A.

0 mm	1 cm	2 cm	3 cm	4 cm	5 cm	6 cm	7 cm	8 cm	9 cm	1 dm 10 cm

1 mm = 0.04 inches	1 cm = 0.39 inches	1 dm = 3.94 inches	1 m = 39.37 inches

0 in.	1 in.	2 in.	3 in.	4 in.

Edible Plant

Ht: 2 m

Rosa canina **Rose Family**

WILD STRAWBERRY

Fragaria vesca / **ROSACEAE   Rose family**

Other Common Names: Woodland Strawberry, Sow-teat Strawberry

Description: *Fragaria:* Low perennial herbs, with leaves, flower stems and runners growing from a scaly rootstalk; leaves alternate, basal, in 3s, with inverted egg-shaped, saw-toothed leaflets; flowers white or pink and fine petaled; fruit is a fleshy, conical berry, reddish. *F. vesca:* Rootstalk short and thick, producing numerous runners; leaflets thin to firm, bright green and strongly  veined above, pale underside and hairy, deeply toothed edges; flowers 3-15 are white or pale pink, 8-13 mm long; fruit succulent.

Range: *Fragaria:* Widely distributed throughout North America in moist open woods, moist banks and hillsides and sandy mountain meadows to 2700 m.

Season: Early blooming, some species as early as February; most fruit ripens in June.

Edible: Primarily the berry.

Preparation: Anything that can be done with a cultivated berry applies to the Wild Strawberry. The wild berry is just smaller and frequently much sweeter and more delicious. In my judgment, there is no finer berry.

Notes of Interest: Isaac Walton wrote of the Wild Strawberry, "Doubtless God could have made a better berry than the strawberry, but doubtless God never did!" The Wild Strawberry is rich in vitamin C.

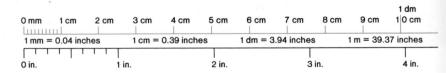

Edible Plant

Ht: 9 cm

WINTER CRESS

Barbarea orthoceras / **CRUCIFERAE**   **Mustard family**

Other Common Names: Yellow Rocket, Scurvy Grass, Wild Mustard

Description: *Barbarea:* Biennial or perennial herb up to
8 dm tall; stems erect, smooth, angular, sometimes
branching; leaves are feather-like divided; medium to
small flowers are yellow. *B. orthoceras:* Semi-suc-
culent, hairless biennial or perennial herb 3-8 dm tall;
conspicuously angled stems; lower leaves 6-11 cm
long, dark green, divided into narrow lobes coming just
short of middle vein, terminal lobe largest, broadly egg-
shaped; upper leaves narrower, coarsely toothed;
small yellow flowers borne in dense clusters; pods,
stout, erect, 2-3 cm long.

Range: *Barbarea:* Widely distributed throughout North America; moist, waste ground, frequently in wooded areas.

Season: Blooms in spring, edible mostly winter and early spring.

Edible: Young leaves, stems and buds.

Preparation: Young leaves, appearing in winter and early spring, are eaten raw or cooked.
Leaves of mature plants (and occasionally even young ones) may be bitter enough to require cooking in two waters. The new buds are harvested and cooked like asparagus or
broccoli.

Notes of Interest: Buds and leaves are both high in vitamin C.

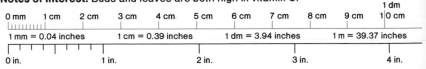

WOOD VIOLET

Viola glabella / **VIOLACEAE**   **Violet family**

Other Common Names: Smooth Woodland Violet

Description: *Viola:* Low annual to perennial herbs with or without a visible stem; leaves simple but greatly varied in shape, mostly broadly heart-shaped; flowers mostly showy, borne singly in leaf axils, are 5-petaled, yellow, white, blue or violet. *V. glabella:* Perennial with leaves and stems growing from a thick scaly rootstalk; basal leaves broadly heart-shaped, 5-9 cm long with long leafstalk; flowering stems erect to 28 cm tall; flowers, 1-3 are deep yellow.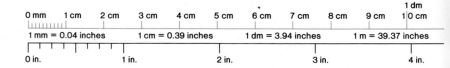

Range: *Viola:* Widely spread throughout North America in moist to dry soils in forests, prairies, mountain slopes, to 2400 m. *V. glabella:* Moist woods, especially near streams, 1500 m to 2300 m.

Season: Blooms May through July. Some species bloom as early as March and others as late as September.

Edible: Blossoms, leaves and stems.

Preparation: In the spring the leaves and flowers are delicious in salads. The dried leaves are a good tea substitute. The leaves may also be used to thicken soups and stews.

Notes of Interest: Violets are a source of vitamins A and C. Both Greeks and Romans used violets in a number of ways — from cosmetic to medicinal applications; its medical uses, however, are dubious.

0 mm	1 cm	2 cm	3 cm	4 cm	5 cm	6 cm	7 cm	8 cm	9 cm	1 dm 10 cm

1 mm = 0.04 inches	1 cm = 0.39 inches	1 dm = 3.94 inches	1 m = 39.37 inches

0 in.	1 in.	2 in.	3 in.	4 in.

YAMPA

Perideridia gairdneri / **UMBELLIFERAE** **Parsley family**

Other Common Names: Squawroot, Yampah, Caraway, Wild Caraway, Ipo, Apah

Description: *Perideridia:* Slender, erect biennial or perennial herb to 1 m tall; leafy stems branching from tuberous root cluster; leaves are compound, with leaflets on each side of leafstalk. *P. gairdneri:* Stem from fleshy tuberous root cluster 4-10 dm high; leaves 1-2 dm long on broad leafstalks, compound or more; few linear grass-like leaflets, 5-15 cm long; basal leaves wither prior to flowering; 3-10 umbrella-like flower heads white or pinkish.

Range: All but one of the 9 species are found in the western United States and Canada; in meadows, open hillsides and generally damp ground, lowlands to 2600 m.

Season: Blooming period from middle to late June through August.

Edible: Primarily the tuberous root cluster.

Preparation: Wash and peel the tubers before boiling (although they are pleasant raw, possessing a sweet, nutty flavor). The tuber can be dried and ground into flour.

Notes of Interest: Yampa rates high in food value and taste along with Camas bulbs and Spring Beauty tubers. Positive identification of this plant is most important in that another plant *(Cicuta bulbifera)* is very similar, but the roots are poisonous. The grass-like leaflets positively identify *P. gairdneri.*

0 mm	1 cm	2 cm	3 cm	4 cm	5 cm	6 cm	7 cm	8 cm	9 cm	1 dm 10 cm

1 mm = 0.04 inches   1 cm = 0.39 inches   1 dm = 3.94 inches   1 m = 39.37 inches

0 in.	1 in.	2 in.	3 in.	4 in.

Edible Plant

Ht: 8 dm

YELLOW BELLS

Fritillaria pudica / **LILIACEAE   Lily family**

Other Common Names: Yellow Fritillary, Rice Root, Mission Bells

Description: *Fritillaria:* Perennial herbs with a simple, erect stem 2-7 dm tall, from scaly bulbs surrounded by numerous rice-like bulblets; leaves alternate or in a circular arrangement, linear to lance-like; flowers single or few, usually large and showy, bell-shaped, nodding. *F. pudica:* Lance-like leaves mostly 2, when more than 2 alternate and arranged in circular manner about stem, 4-16 cm long; flowers, mostly 1, occasionally 2 or 3, turning from green to yellow to orange-brown with age.

Range: *Fritillaria:* A widely varied habitat in the western United States and B.C., Canada. *F. pudica:* Found in open grasslands, grassy slopes and in open dry woods from 1200-1300 m.

Season: Blooms March through May.

Edible: Bulb.

Preparation: The bulbs can be eaten raw, but are good cooked or steamed; however do not overcook as the bulb is tender and delicate. It is nearly rice-like in taste. Indians of the Northwest dried these bulbs and pounded them for flour.

Notes of Interest: Although *Fritillaria* is not an endangered plant species, it is among those we discourage harvesting for aesthetic reasons.

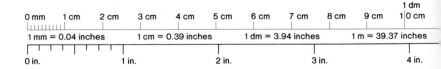

									1 dm
0 mm	1 cm	2 cm	3 cm	4 cm	5 cm	6 cm	7 cm	8 cm	9 cm 10 cm

1 mm = 0.04 inches   1 cm = 0.39 inches   1 dm = 3.94 inches   1 m = 39.37 inches

0 in.	1 in.	2 in.	3 in.	4 in.

Ht: 5 dm

YELLOW NUT GRASS

Cyperus esculentus / **CYPERACEAE** **Sedge family**

Other Common Names: Nut Grass

Description: *Cyperus:* Annual or perennial grass-like plants 4 cm to 8 dm high; stem, slender or stout, pithy, triangular in cross section; leaves basal or near base, long, grass-like, in 3 rows; several upper leaves just below flower cluster; flower cluster spike-like. *C. esculentus:* Stout stemmed perennial sedge 3-8 dm tall; tuber bearing rootstalks, slender, numerous; tubers round; light green leaves, rough-edged, those above extending to height of or higher than flower clusters; straw-colored flower clusters in spikelets are numerous.

Range: *Cyperus:* Widely distributed throughout most of North America; moist fields (but not swamps) and stream banks.

Season: Harvest whenever identified.

Edible: Nut-like tubers.

Preparation: In sandy soil tubers harvested by pulling up plants, otherwise some digging and searching may be required when plant is found in more sticky soil. Nut-like tubers are pared, cleaned and dried of rinse water. They are eaten raw or roasted, or roasted to a dark brown, ground and brewed like coffee.

Notes of Interest: This plant is cultivated in the southern United States and in some area of Europe.

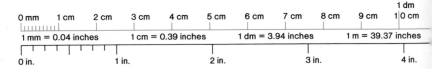

0 mm	1 cm	2 cm	3 cm	4 cm	5 cm	6 cm	7 cm	8 cm	9 cm	1 dm 1|0 cm

1 mm = 0.04 inches   1 cm = 0.39 inches   1 dm = 3.94 inches   1 m = 39.37 inches

0 in.		1 in.		2 in.		3 in.		4 in.

YELLOW POND LILY

Nuphar polysepalum / **NYMPHAEACEAE** **Water-lily family**

Other Common Names: Wokas (also spelled Wakas), Spatterdock

Description: Aquatic, perennial herb with large and long cylindric rootstalk; large, dark, floating, somewhat shiny leaves are round-oval or heart-shaped 1-3 dm wide; deep yellow cup-like flowers mostly at water surface.

Range: Various sub-species found widely distributed throughout North America; small lakes or ponds from low to relatively high altitudes.

Season: Blooming period, May to August; seed harvested mid-summer to autumn.

Edible: Seed and rootstalks.

Preparation: Globe-like seed cups are harvested and the seeds removed. Seeds may be pan heated until they burst open similar to popcorn; in fact, taste is similar. Seeds are also cooked, mashed and winnowed to make flour. Starchy, sweet tasting rootstalks, too, are good eating. They are boiled or roasted, then peeled and core (pith) is eaten. The cooked, dried core may also be ground and used as flour.

Notes of Interest: Wokas, Indian name for this plant, were an important part of the Northwest Indian diet. To the Klamath Indians the "in the thumb month" (harvest time) initiated huge ceremonial dances in behalf of their greatest annual food harvest.

0 mm　1 cm　2 cm	3 cm　4 cm　5 cm	6 cm　7 cm　8 cm	1 dm 9 cm　10 cm
1 mm = 0.04 inches	1 cm = 0.39 inches	1 dm = 3.94 inches	1 m = 39.37 inches
0 in.	1 in.	2 in.	3 in.　4 in.

Edible Plant

Dia: 3 dm

Nuphar polysepalum **Water-lily Family**

POISONOUS PLANTS

(Causing Internal Poisoning)

ABOUT POISONOUS PLANTS

Internal poisoning caused through the ingestion of poisonous plant material is a serious matter. Although most plants are non toxic, mildly toxic, or only toxic to certain individuals, a few plants are extremely poisonous with a small number considered deadly poisonous. In the case of some plants (i.e., Destroying Angel, *Amanita verna)* only an infinitesimal amount can be lethal; there is no known remedy and the prognosis is for an agonizing death.

Once again, we feel compelled to restate three important rules before considering any plant as a food source.

1. If you cannot positively identify the plant **do not consider using it as a food source.**

2. **There is no such thing as a safe, general edibility test.** In the case of a small number of plants the taste and immediate effect may be pleasing and positive, but there may be a cumulative negative effect that may occur over a period of time (i.e., the Bracken Fern, *Pteridium aquilinum,* commonly referred to as "fiddlehead" in its early stages, which has been found to contain toxins which are potentially carcinogetic if consumed regularly over a long period).

3. Because you see an animal eating a certain plant does not mean that it is fit for humans. Horses eat poison ivy, squirrels eat all mushrooms, bears eat baneberry, and birds eat plant seeds containing strychnine.

When a plant poisoning or suspected plant poisoning occurs, it is a helpful practice to harvest the suspected plant. When medical help becomes available, the positive identification of the plant will aid in administering the proper treatment for the toxin(s) involved.

Perhaps the greatest single source for contemporary drugs comes from the chemical compounds found in or derived from plants. It is a paradox that a substantial number of these are derived from poisonous plants (i.e., the drug digitalis extracted from Foxglove, *Digitalis purpurea,* is used in treating certain types of heart problems). Nevertheless, in no instance should poisonous plants be eaten in their natural form.

In that the scope of the treatments prescribed in this book are mostly limited to those which reasonably may be applied "in field," we do not discuss treatments or procedures which require a medical doctor or his drugs and equipment.

While professional medical experience, drugs, and equipment can minimize the effects of some of the toxins described here, it is unfortunate that all too often the chemical which will neutralize a particular toxin is not known. Whether in the hospital or in the wilderness, treatment is often supportive, allowing the body to recover in its own time with as much help as possible. The lack of even the supportive chemicals and equipment in the wilderness increases the risk of injury or death due to poisoning. It also increases the importance of being aware of which plants are poisonous.

The plants and fungi selected for this section (this is not a complete listing of poisonous plants found in North America) were chosen on the basis of two or more of the following criteria:

1. The common appearance and / or the generally wide distribution (range) of the genus or species.

2. The plants which account for the largest number of poisonings.

3. The plants which have edible look-alikes.

4. The severity of the human body's reaction to the plant toxin(s).

Prevention is the best alternative to treatment. Probably the greatest specific value of this section will be that with its use a number of the poisonous plants found in North America can be recognized and avoided.

① **FOXGLOVE**

② *Digitalis purpurea* ③ **SCROPHULARIACEAE** ④ **Figwort family**

⑤ **Other Common Names:** Dead Men's Bells, Digitalis, Fairy Caps, Fairy's Glove, Fairy Thimbles.

⑥ **Description:** Erect biennial with mostly one, occasionally more, sturdy flowering stems to 15 dm; leaves lanceolate to ovate-lanceolate, alternate and crenate, with prominent lateral veins; flowers drooping, bell-shaped, tubular, 3-8 cm long in tall, showy terminal spikes; flowers range in color from white to purple, sometimes yellow; fruit a dry capsule.

⑦ **Range:** Native to Europe; commonly cultivated for ornament. Prevalent in disturbed rich soils in open areas (ie., logged-off areas, burns, dry hilly pastures, and along roadsides from British Columbia to northern California and occasionally east to the Atlantic.

⑧ **Season:** Blooms in early to mid-summer depending upon location and elevation. The peak flowering period is during July; fruit ripens beginning in mid-summer.

⑨ **Toxic Parts & Toxins:** All parts, especially the green leaves. The plant contains numerous glycosides, several of which are cardiac stimulants. Digitoxin, one of the most powerful of these, is extremely poisonous.

⑩ **Poison Symptoms:** Nausea, vomiting, diarrhea, abdominal pain, headache, irregular pulse, tremors and convulsions.

⑪ **Treatment:** Seek immediate medical attention — a life threatening emergency. Quickly induce vomiting. Administer drinking water/vomiting sessions until vomit is free of plant material. Cardiac symptoms usually occur within 2-4 hours with maximum effect in about 8-10 hours. Some symptoms may persist for two to three weeks.

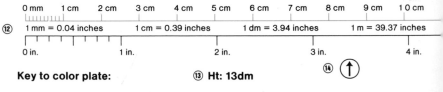

⑫

| 0 mm | 1 cm | 2 cm | 3 cm | 4 cm | 5 cm | 6 cm | 7 cm | 8 cm | 9 cm | 1 dm 10 cm |

1 mm = 0.04 inches　　1 cm = 0.39 inches　　1 dm = 3.94 inches　　1 m = 39.37 inches

| 0 in. | 1 in. | 2 in. | 3 in. | 4 in. |

Key to color plate: ⑬ **Ht: 13dm** ⑭ (↑)

EXPLANATORY NOTES

Poisonous Plant

① Widely accepted common plant name.

② Botanical (scientific) plant name. The first name (i.e., *Digitalis*) is that of the plant genus (the main subdivision within a particular plant family). The second name (i.e., *purpurea*) is the plant's specific name.

③ The scientific family name.

④ The common family name.

⑤ Synonym(s) or nickname(s) by which the plant is known.

⑥ Distinguishing characteristics and detailed description of the plant in the color plate.

⑦ Indicates the broad range and habitat appearance of the genus (occasionally refers to the specific plant in the color plate).

⑧ Refers to the blooming period and / or fruit appearance.

⑨ Notes those parts of the plant which are poisonous and names the primary poisoning agent(s).

⑩ Lists the poison symptoms. These are given in the order they frequently appear. Some of these symptoms will vary from individual to individual based upon the amount of the plant ingested, the part of the plant ingested, and the age and weight of the individual.

⑪ Field treatment for internal poisoning and external poisoning (in the case of contact poison plants). In nearly all cases of internal poisoning medical help should be sought as quickly as possible.

⑫ An equivalency scale for easy translation of the metric measures given in the plant description to the customary (inch) scale.

⑬ Refers to the height of the plant in the color plate.

⑭ Indicates the top of the color plate.

AMERICAN MISTLETOE

Phoradendron flavescens / **LORANTHACEAE** **Mistletoe family**

Other Common Names: Mistletoe

Description: Small parasitic, freely branching fleshy shrubs with jointed stems; this species prefers oak; plant finely velvety-hairy on new growth; evergreen leaves 10-40 mm, opposite, ovate to obovate in shape, leaves stemmed; flowers more or less sunken in short jointed spikes 1-5 cm long; fruit a sticky white berry.

Range: New Jersey to southern Missouri; south to Florida, Texas, and New Mexico; also in western Oregon.

Season: Plants available throughout year; fruit persists into winter.

Toxic Parts & Toxins: All parts, especially the berries, are poisonous. The berries contain beta-phenylethylamine and tryamine.

Poison Symptoms: Stomach and intestinal pain with diarrhea, slow pulse, decrease in blood pressure, weakened heart beat, and collapse. Death can occur within a few hours. Other symptoms include nausea and vomiting, nervousness, difficulty in breathing, delirium, hallucinations, convulsions, and dilation of pupils.

Treatment: Seek immediate medical assistance — a life threatening emergency. Induce vomiting followed by drinking water / vomiting sessions until free of plant material. If respiration and / or heart fail, give CPR, continuing until respiration is restored.

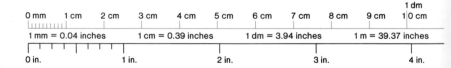

0 mm	1 cm	2 cm	3 cm	4 cm	5 cm	6 cm	7 cm	8 cm	9 cm	1 dm 10 cm

1 mm = 0.04 inches   1 cm = 0.39 inches   1 dm = 3.94 inches   1 m = 39.37 inches

0 in.   1 in.   2 in.   3 in.   4 in.

Ht: 4.5 dm

BANEBERRY

Actaea rubra (A. arguta) / **RANUNCULACEAE** **Buttercup family**

Other Common Names: Red Baneberry, Cohosh.

Description: Erect perennial herbs, 4-10 dm tall from a thick rhizome; leaves 2-3 times ternate and more or less pinnately divided, leaflets with toothed margins; flowers inconspicuous, white (often with purple tinge), in terminal racemes; fruit a berry with smooth seeds, generally red although occasional white berried plants may be found.

Range: In moist woods throughout much of Canada and U.S. but generally not common.

Season: Flowers in spring, fruit in summer.

Toxic Parts & Toxins: All parts, but especially the roots, berries, and sap. Poisoning apparently caused by an essential oil.

Poison Symptoms: Severe gastroenteritis, vomiting, diarrhea, headache, dizziness, shock, increased pulse, delirium, visual hallucinations, circulatory failure. Death can occur. As few as six berries can cause severe poisoning.

Treatment: Seek immediate medical assistance — a life threatening emergency. If not immediately available, induce vomiting **after** giving water or milk to dilute tissue damaging toxins. Continue liquid / vomiting sessions until free of plant material. Administer activated charcoal if available. After cleaning the stomach, egg whites or milk may be given to soothe stomach. If heart failure occurs, administer CPR. Continue until medical assistance is available.

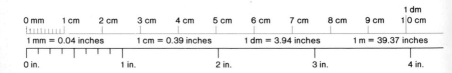

0 mm	1 cm	2 cm	3 cm	4 cm	5 cm	6 cm	7 cm	8 cm	9 cm	1 dm 10 cm

1 mm = 0.04 inches   1 cm = 0.39 inches   1 dm = 3.94 inches   1 m = 39.37 inches

| 0 in. | | 1 in. | | 2 in. | | 3 in. | | 4 in. |

Ht: 6 dm

Actaea rubra **Buttercup Family**

BELLADONNA

Atropa belladonna / **SOLANACEAE** **Nightshade family**

Other Common Names: Deadly Nightshade, Devil's Cherries.

Description: Bushy, branching, herbaceous perennial 6-20 dm high; stem is annual, stout, purple in color, dividing mostly to three just above the ground, then freely branching; leaves dull, dark green, 7-25 cm long, entire, ovate, alternate but appearing to be in pairs with one leaf of each pair substantially larger; five-pointed, bell-shaped flower, single, purplish, from leaf axil; fruit (berry) surrounded by remains of flower is smooth, purple or black, 10-15 mm across.

Range: Native to Europe, this plant is cultivated and thus likely to be found escaped and wild throughout much of North America.

Season: Flowers appear early to mid-summer, blooming until late summer. The berry ripens in September.

Toxic Parts & Toxins: The berries, leaves, and roots contain atropine and other related alkaloids. As few as three berries may kill a child.

Poison Symptoms: Fever, rapid heartbeat, dilation of pupils, difficulty in speaking; skin becomes flushed, dry, and hot. Amnesia may occur in the intoxication period.

Treatment: Seek immediate medical assistance — a life threatening emergency. Quickly induce vomiting. Administer drinking water / vomiting sessions until vomit is free of plant material. Cardiac symptoms usually occur within 2-4 hours with maximum effect in about 8-10 hours. Some symptoms may persist for two to three weeks.

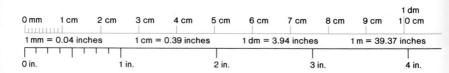

									1 dm
0 mm	1 cm	2 cm	3 cm	4 cm	5 cm	6 cm	7 cm	8 cm	9 cm	10 cm

1 mm = 0.04 inches   1 cm = 0.39 inches   1 dm = 3.94 inches   1 m = 39.37 inches

0 in.   1 in.   2 in.   3 in.   4 in.

Poisonous Plant

Ht: 1 m

Atropa belladonna   **Nightshade Family**

BLACK HENBANE

Hyoscyamus niger / **SOLANACEAE Nightshade family**

Other Common Names: Common Henbane, Hyoscyamus, Hog's Bean.

Description: An annual or biennial, coarse, hairy herb, 3-12 dm tall; leaves 7-20 cm long, oblong, irregularly toothed to pinnatifid, lower leaves sessile or with sessile or with short stalks, upper leaves clasping the stem; flower bell-shaped, greenish-yellow to yellowish-white with purple veins, about 3 cm wide and long; fruit a globe-shape capsule surrounded by the green flower sepals that continue growing as the fruit matures.

Range: Native to Europe, now found in southern Canada and northern United States; common in northern Rocky Mountain states. Found in dry soil in waste areas and along roadbeds.

Season: Flowers from June through September; fruit ripens starting in late summer.

Toxic Parts & Toxins: All parts of the plant contain atropine, hyoscyamine, hyoscine and related alkaloids.

Poison Symptoms: Increased salivation, headache, nausea, rapid pulse, convulsions, coma, and death. Amnesia may occur in the intoxication period.

Treatment: Seek immediate medical assistance — a life threatening emergency. Quickly induce vomiting. Administer drinking water / vomiting sessions until vomit is free of plant material. Cardiac symptoms usually occur within 2-4 hours with maximum effect in about 8-10 hours. Some symptoms may persist for two to three weeks.

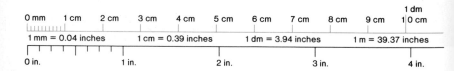

BLACK LOCUST

Robinia pseudoacacia / **LEGUMINOSAE   Pea family**

Other Common Names: Yellow Locust, Black Acacia, False Acacia.

Description: A large tree (to 25 m) with generally rough almost black bark; leaves alternate, odd-pinnately compound with 7-25 leaflets, each leaflet oval or elliptical, entire smooth margin; 2 usually stout spines at the base of the leaf stalk; flowers pea-like, white, fragrant, 30-70 in a drooping raceme 10-14 cm long; pods flat, reddish brown, 6-10 cm long.

Range: Native to the eastern U.S. from Pennsylvania to Oklahoma, Louisiana, and Georgia; planted further north and westward into Iowa; also widely naturalized in the Pacific Northwest.

Season: Flowers in late spring to early summer; fruit persists into winter.

Toxic Parts & Toxins: The bark, leaves, and seeds contain two toxalbumins, robin and phasin, and a glycoside, robitin.

Poison Symptoms: Anorexia, nausea, vomiting (may contain blood and mucus), diarrhea, dullness and depression, weak and irregular pulse, coldness of arms and legs, and marked dilation of pupils. In severe cases breathing difficulty may occur.

Treatment: Induce vomiting followed by drinking water / vomiting sessions until free of plant material. Give fluids to help prevent dehydration. Administer 5-15 grams of sodium bicarbonate (bicarbonate of soda or baking soda) daily. Human fatalities rare but children more susceptible. Recovery takes several days or weeks.

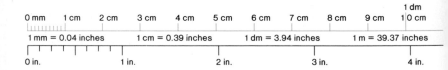

0 mm	1 cm	2 cm	3 cm	4 cm	5 cm	6 cm	7 cm	8 cm	9 cm	1 dm 10 cm

1 mm = 0.04 inches	1 cm = 0.39 inches	1 dm = 3.94 inches	1 m = 39.37 inches

0 in.	1 in.	2 in.	3 in.	4 in.

Poisonous Plant

Ht: 18 m

Robinia pseudoacacia **Pea Family**

BLEEDING HEART

Dicentra formosa / **FUMARIACEAE   Fumitory family**

Other Common Names: Dutchman's Breeches, Dicentra

Description: Plants 15-60 cm tall; rhizomatous; leaves ternately divided, the ultimate segments deeply lobed and very narrow; flowers paniculate, usually deep pink, outer petals rounded-saccate at base; fruit a capsule.

Range: The West Coast from the Cascade Mountains to the Pacific Ocean and British Columbia to northern California.

Season: Flowers in spring.

Toxic Parts & Toxins: All parts of the plant contain toxic isoquinoline-type alkaloids including protopine, protoberberine, and aporphine.

Poison Symptoms: Trembling, staggering, convulsions, and labored breathing. Large amounts can be fatal.

Treatment: Seek medical attention. Induce vomiting followed by drinking water/vomiting sessions until free of plant material. Administer activated charcoal if available. If respiratory failure occurs, begin CPR and maintain until respiration is restored.

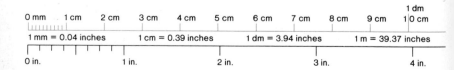

| 0 mm | 1 cm | 2 cm | 3 cm | 4 cm | 5 cm | 6 cm | 7 cm | 8 cm | 9 cm | 1 dm 10 cm |

1 mm = 0.04 inches   1 cm = 0.39 inches   1 dm = 3.94 inches   1 m = 39.37 inches

| 0 in. | 1 in. | 2 in. | 3 in. | 4 in. |

BRACKEN FERN

Pteridium aquilinum / **POLYPODIACEAE Fern family**

Other Common Names: Brake Fern.

Description: Medium-sized to large ferns with elongated, black-skinned, underground rhizomes; each "fern" an individual leaf; stalk coarse and firm; leaf blade about thrice compound, ultimate segments numerous, crowded, and directly attached to leaf branches; sori along leaflet margins, protected by inrolled leaf margin.

Range: Throughout most of North America except in areas of climatic extremes.

Season: From spring to first hard frost.

Toxic Parts & Toxins: The entire plant contains compounds resulting in two toxic syndromes. The first is caused by a thiamine destroying enzyme, the second by a carcinogenic tannin.

Poison Symptoms: Bracken toxins ordinarily do not produce acute symptoms in humans. Thiamine deficiency generally does not occur unless bracken comprises over 20% of the diet. The tannin's carcinogenic effect will not be apparent until long after the plant was eaten and probably does not pose a significant risk from occasional consumption of a small serving of fiddleheads. However, regular use of bracken for food appears to present significant risk of precipitating a variety of cancers.

Treatment: In general, insufficient material will be consumed to require any active treatment. In the extremely unlikely event that thiamine deficiency should occur in a human, massive doses of thiamine should prove successful as therapy. Vomiting can be induced to remove the plant, especially if large amounts have been consumed. Milk may help protect against the activity of the tannin.

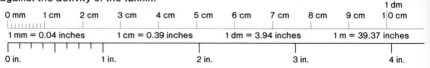

Poisonous Plant

Ht: 4 dm

DEATH CAMAS

Zigadenus paniculatus / **LILIACEAE**   **Lily family**

Other Common Names: Zigadenus, Zygadene.

Description: Perennial herbs from underground bulbs; stems simple, leafy at base with reduced leaves or membraneous bracts above; leaves linear, generally hairless, often with a bluish waxy coating; flowers in a panicle, white to yellow-green, saucer to shallowly cup shaped, withering but persistent; fruit a 3-sectioned capsule. May be distinguished from onions by the lack of an onion or garlic odor.

Range: From northern Washington east of the Cascades south to Sierran, California, Arizona and northwest New Mexico; east to central Montana, western Wyoming, and western Colorado. Other species extend east to the Dakotas and Nebraska, south to northern Mexico, north into western Canada; also west of the Cascades.

Season: Flowers in spring, bulbs available and poisonous all year.

Toxic Parts & Toxins: The entire plant, especially the bulb, is highly poisonous. Toxins include the alkaloids zygadenine and veratrine.

Poison Symptoms: Excessive watering of mouth, muscular weakness, slow heartbeat, low blood pressure (high blood pressure may occur when large doses are taken), subnormal temperature, nausea, vomiting, diarrhea, stomach pains, difficulty in breathing, visual disturbances, coma, sometimes death.

Treatment: Seek immediate medical assistance — a life threatening emergency. Induce vomiting followed by water drinking / vomiting sessions until free of plant material. Administer activated charcoal if available. In severe cases CPR may be necessary.

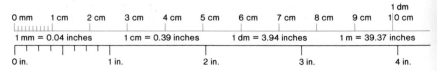

0 mm	1 cm	2 cm	3 cm	4 cm	5 cm	6 cm	7 cm	8 cm	9 cm	1 dm 10 cm

| 1 mm = 0.04 inches | 1 cm = 0.39 inches | 1 dm = 3.94 inches | 1 m = 39.37 inches |

| 0 in. | 1 in. | 2 in. | 3 in. | 4 in. |

DESTROYING ANGEL

Amanita verna, A. virosa, A. bisporigera / **AMANITACEAE**   **Amanita family**

Other Common Names: Death Angel.

Description: Differences in these three species nearly indiscernible, but all are deadly. Pure white cap is 3-10 cm broad, conic to egg-shaped when young, generally slightly convex to flat in age. Flesh is firm and white; gills are white, free from the stalk; spores white. Stalk 14-24 cm long, 10-23 mm wide, white, enlarging gradually to a bulbous base. A volva or death cup is present at the base of the stalk.

Range: Occur under hardwood and mixed woods, especially in aspen and birch forests of northern U.S. and in oak forests of the South. *A. pholloides* is known from California, Oregon, New Jersey, and Pennsylvania.

Season: Spring and summer, but mostly autumn.

Toxic Parts & Toxins: All parts of these mushrooms are DEADLY POISONOUS! Toxins are complex polypeptide molecules known as phallotoxins and amatoxins.

Poison Symptoms: Occur suddenly 6-15 hours after consumption. Extreme pain, profuse vomiting, lethargy, and distorted vision. Some hours later the slower amatoxins also take effect. In 3-8 days severe pain, peripheral circulatory collapse, hepatic coma, and death. Brain damage may also occur along with permanent liver damage in survivors.

Treatment: DEADLY POISONOUS. Seek immediate medical assistance — a life threatening emergency. The symptoms are delayed, making the application of first aid often useless. If the error is caught quickly, induce vomiting followed by water drinking / vomiting sessions until free of plant material.

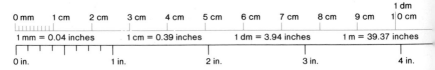

Poisonous Plant

Ht: 1 dm

FALSE HELLEBORE

Veratrum californicum / **LILIACEAE Lily family**

Other Common Names: Skunk Cabbage, Corn Lily.

Description: Tall perennial herb (to over 2 m) from a thick rhizome; stem simple with numerous broad, coarsely veined, alternate leaves; leaves more or less ovate to elliptic in shape; flowers in dense panicles, the branches crowded, spreading to ascending, not drooping; flowers, white to greenish; fruit are 3-lobed capsules.

Range: Western U.S. east to Montana and south to Mexico. *V. viride* (Indian-poke) occurs in Alaska to Oregon, across Canada to Quebec, and south to North Carolina.

Season: Depending on location, flowers from early to mid summer.

Toxic Parts & Toxins: The entire plant is poisonous. False Hellebores contain toxic alkaloids including veratrosine, veradridene, and veratrine.

Poison Symptoms: Watering of the mouth, vomiting, diarrhea, stomach pains, general paralysis, and spasms. Severe cases may cause shallow difficult breathing, slow pulse, depressed heart action, lowered temperature, convulsions, and death. Hallucinations and headache have also been reported. *V. californicum* also causing low blood pressure.

Treatment: Seek immediate medical assistance — a life threatening emergency. Induce vomiting followed by water drinking / vomiting sessions until free of plant material. Administer activated charcoal if available. If breathing or circulation fail, apply CPR.

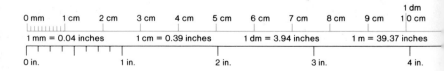

| | | | | | | | | | 1 dm |
| 0 mm | 1 cm | 2 cm | 3 cm | 4 cm | 5 cm | 6 cm | 7 cm | 8 cm | 9 cm | 10 cm |

| 1 mm = 0.04 inches | 1 cm = 0.39 inches | 1 dm = 3.94 inches | 1 m = 39.37 inches |

| 0 in. | 1 in. | 2 in. | 3 in. | 4 in. |

Poisonous Plant

Ht: 8 dm

FLY AMANITA

Amanita muscaria / **AMANITACEAE** **Amanita family**

Other Common Names: Fly Agaric.

Description: Cap 8-25 cm broad, red to orange or yellow, more or less covered with whitish warts or patches of outer (universal) veil tissue; the stalk is white with an annulus or ring of partial veil tissue about ¾ up the stalk; the outer veil is intergrown with the tissue of the bulb (hence no free volva or death cup); gills crowded, broad, white or cream colored, free from the stalk; spores are white.

Range: Widely distributed in forested areas throughout North America.

Season: Spring and late summer through fall.

Toxic Parts & Toxins: The entire mushroom is poisonous. Toxins include ibotenic acid, muscimol, and related compounds.

Poison Symptoms: Symptoms occur rapidly and are severe yet rarely fatal. Increased secretions of the salivary and other glands, perspiration, frequently severe gastro-intestinal disturbances; breathing may be labored; pupils rarely respond to light. Typical scenario: light sleep 2 hours followed by elation, hyperactivity, and/or auditory hallucinations for 3-4 hours or longer, followed by death-like sleep from which patient awakens without symptoms or even memory of poisoning.

Treatment: Seek immediate medical attention. Atropine, recommended in older works as an antidote, should not be given. It will aggravate rather than help ameliorate symptoms. Induce vomiting followed by water drinking/vomiting sessions until free of plant material.

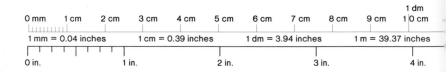

									1 dm
0 mm	1 cm	2 cm	3 cm	4 cm	5 cm	6 cm	7 cm	8 cm	9 cm	1 0 cm

1 mm = 0.04 inches	1 cm = 0.39 inches	1 dm = 3.94 inches	1 m = 39.37 inches

0 in.	1 in.	2 in.	3 in.	4 in.

Poisonous Plant

Ht: 8 cm

FOXGLOVE

Digitalis purpurea / **SCROPHULARIACEAE**   **Figwort family**

Other Common Names: Dead Men's Bells, Digitalis, Fairy Caps, Fairy's Glove, Fairy Thimbles.

Description: Erect biennial with mostly one, occasionally more, sturdy flowering stems to 15 dm; leaves lanceolate to ovate-lanceolate, alternate and crenate, with prominent lateral veins; flowers drooping, bell-shaped, tubular, 3-8 cm long in tall, showy terminal spikes; flowers range in color from white to purple, sometimes yellow; fruit a dry capsule.

Range: Native to Europe; commonly cultivated for ornament. Prevalent in disturbed rich soils in open areas (ie., logged-off areas, burns, dry hilly pastures, and along roadsides from British Columbia to northern California and occasionally east to the Atlantic.

Season: Blooms in early to mid-summer depending upon location and elevation. The peak flowering period is during July; fruit ripens beginning in mid-summer.

Toxic Parts & Toxins: All parts, especially the green leaves. The plant contains numerous glycosides, several of which are cardiac stimulants. Digitoxin, one of the most powerful o these, is extremely poisonous.

Poison Symptoms: Nausea, vomiting, diarrhea, abdominal pain, headache, irregula pulse, tremors, and convulsions.

Treatment: Seek immediate medical assistance — a life threatening emergency. Quickly induce vomiting. Administer drinking water / vomiting sessions until vomit is free of plant ma terial. Cardiac symptoms usually occur within 2-4 hours with maximum effect in about 8-10 hours. Some symptoms may persist for two to three weeks.

0 mm	1 cm	2 cm	3 cm	4 cm	5 cm	6 cm	7 cm	8 cm	9 cm	1 dm 1|0 cm

1 mm = 0.04 inches	1 cm = 0.39 inches	1 dm = 3.94 inches	1 m = 39.37 inches

0 in.	1 in.	2 in.	3 in.	4 in.

Ht: 1 m

JIMSON WEED

Datura stramonium / **SOLANACEAE Nightshade family**

Other Common Names: Datura, Devil's Apple, Devil's Trumpet, Thorn Apple, Jamestown Weed.

Description: Large, coarse, freely branching, annual herb 10-17 dm; stem erect, stout, hollow, leafy, smooth, fork-like branching, and yellow-green or purple in color; leaves large, angular-ovate, coarsely-toothed margin with pronounced points and strongly veined, grey-green upper surface and lighter beneath, 10-20 cm; five pointed flower is funnel-shaped, white or purple, 7-10 cm long from short stems at leaf axil; fruit a capsule, ovate, spiny, green, 3-5 cm long.

Range: Throughout most of North America except in the cold or Arctic areas. In waste places, disturbed ground, along roadsides.

Season: Flowers can appear throughout the summer, seed capsules from August onward.

Toxic Parts & Toxins: All parts of the plant contain atropine, hyoscyamine, hyoscine (scopolamine), alkaloids. The seeds and leaves are the most toxic. Very small amounts (4-5 grams) can kill a child.

Poison Symptoms: Exaggerated thirst, dilation of the pupils, dry mouth, red skin, nausea, rapid pulse, high blood pressure, headache, hallucinations, delirium, convulsions, coma, and death. Amnesia may occur in the intoxication period.

Treatment: Seek immediate medical assistance — a life threatening emergency. Quickly induce vomiting. Administer drinking water / vomiting sessions until vomit is free of plant material. Cardiac symptoms usually occur within 2-4 hours with maximum effect in about 8-10 hours. Some symptoms may persist for two to three weeks.

0 mm	1 cm	2 cm	3 cm	4 cm	5 cm	6 cm	7 cm	8 cm	9 cm	1 dm 10 cm

1 mm = 0.04 inches	1 cm = 0.39 inches	1 dm = 3.94 inches	1 m = 39.37 inches

0 in.	1 in.	2 in.	3 in.	4 in.

Datura stramonium   **Nightshade Family**

LARKSPUR

Delphinium spp. / **RANUNCULACEAE**   **Buttercup family**

Other Common Names: Delphinium, Staggerweed.

Description: Annual or perennial herbs to 12 dm tall; leaves finely palmately divided on long stems; flowers generally blue or purple but may be white, pink, or rose color in a terminal raceme, each flower with a characteristic spur projecting from the upper backside; fruit a many seeded follicle.

Range: Throughout the U.S. but more common in the western states. Several species are cultivated as ornamentals in gardens.

Season: Flowers spring to mid-summer depending on locality, species, and elevation.

Toxic Parts & Toxins: The seeds and young plants are the most toxic, but all ages and parts of the plant should be considered dangerous. Toxins include the alkaloids delphinine, delphineidine, and ajacine.

Poison Symptoms: Burning sensation of mouth and skin, upset stomach, nausea, constipation, nervous symptoms, depression, convulsions, low blood pressure, weak pulse, and respiratory paralysis. May be quickly fatal if consumed in large amounts. Possible contact dermatitis in susceptible people.

Treatment: Seek medical assistance — a life threatening emergency. Induce vomiting followed by drinking water / vomiting sessions until free of plant material. In the event of heart or breathing failure initiate CPR and continue until help arrives.

| | | | | | | | | | 1 dm |
| 0 mm | 1 cm | 2 cm | 3 cm | 4 cm | 5 cm | 6 cm | 7 cm | 8 cm | 9 cm | 10 cm |

1 mm = 0.04 inches   1 cm = 0.39 inches   1 dm = 3.94 inches   1 m = 39.37 inches

0 in.   1 in.   2 in.   3 in.   4 in.

LUPINE

Lupinus spp. / **LEGUMINOSAE   Pea family**

Other Common Names: A variety of names exist for the various species in this genus, but almost all contain "Lupine" as part of the name.

Description: Annual to perennial herbs (some species shrubs); height varies with species from 1 dm to 1 m or more; some in cultivation; leaves palmately compound with (3) 5-17 narrow leaflets. Flowers usually showy, pea-like, generally in terminal racemes, but sometimes whorled, blue, purplish, white, or yellow, sometimes pink in cultivated forms; fruit a legume, pods flattened.

Range: Lupines occur throughout the U.S. but are much more common in the western states.

Season: Flowers from mid-spring to early summer but varies depending on the species, locality, and elevation. Pods ripen in summer among the low elevation species.

Toxic Parts & Toxins: Alkaloids are found in the foliage, but the highest concentration is in the seeds. Several alkaloids have been isolated from species of lupine. Most are quinolizidine alkaloids, however some piperidine and other types of alkaloids have been found.

Poison Symptoms: Paralysis, weak pulse, depressed breathing, convulsions.

Treatment: Seek prompt medical assistance. Immediately induce vomiting followed by drinking water/vomiting sessions until free of plant material. Administration of activated charcoal may be helpful if available. If breathing becomes seriously depressed, initiate CPR and continue until help arrives.

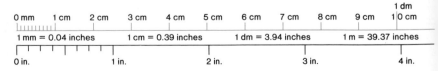

MONKSHOOD

Aconitum columbianum / **RANUNCULACEAE** **Buttercup family**

Other Common Names: Wolfsbane, Aconite.

Description: Perennial herb up to 2 m tall; leaves alternate, petioled, palmately divided segments with pointed tips; flowers dark bluish purple, white, or greenish yellow, the upper sepal forming a prominent hood; unlike Larkspur the flowers lack spurs; fruit of 3-5 follicles

Range: Alaska south to California, east to Alberta and south to New Mexico. Other species occur in the eastern U.S.

Season: Flowers in summer.

Toxic Parts & Toxins: All parts of the plant contain several monobasic alkaloids including aconitine and aconine. Plants are most poisonous in the preflowering state. The roots and seeds are especially toxic.

Poison Symptoms: Symptoms include burning sensation of mouth and skin, nausea, intensive vomiting and diarrhea, muscular weakness and spasms, weak and irregular pulse, respiratory paralysis, dimness of vision, low blood pressure, convulsions, and death usually within a few hours (or within minutes to four days). As little as two grams of the root can be lethal. Avoid prolonged contact with the leaves as toxins may be absorbed through the skin.

Treatment: Seek immediate medical assistance — a life threatening emergency. Immediately induce vomiting followed by drinking water / vomiting sessions until free of plant material. Give activated charcoal if available. If respiratory or circulatory failure occurs, administer CPR. Aconite poisoning is a serious medical emergency.

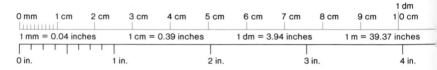

| 0 mm | 1 cm | 2 cm | 3 cm | 4 cm | 5 cm | 6 cm | 7 cm | 8 cm | 9 cm | 1 dm 10 cm |

| 1 mm = 0.04 inches | 1 cm = 0.39 inches | 1 dm = 3.94 inches | 1 m = 39.37 inches |

| 0 in. | 1 in. | 2 in. | 3 in. | 4 in. |

Ht: 1 m

POISON HEMLOCK

Conium maculatum / **UMBELLIFERAE**   **Parsley family**

Other Common Names: Poison Parsley, Spotted Hemlock.

Description: Tall, sturdy, hollow stemmed, much-branching biennial 1-3 m with lower stems distinctively blotched (spotted) with purple; numerous leaves tripinnate, forming elegant lacy triangular fern-like outlines diminishing in size with plant height; small white flowers borne in compound umbels, umbellets 2-5 cm; fruit (seed) 2-2.5 mm with prominent, often raised and almost winged longitudinal ridges. Plant has a bitter taste and mousy odor.

Range: Native to Europe, now found throughout the U.S. and Canada along roadsides and stream borders and in waste ground mostly below 1300 m.

Season: Flowers in early summer; fruit ripens in late summer.

Toxic Parts & Toxins: Poison hemlock contains at least five closely related alkaloids: coniine, N-methyl coniine, conhydrine, coniceine, and pseudo-conhydrine. The entire plant is extremely poisonous, especially the seeds.

Poison Symptoms: Burning sensation in the mouth and throat, vomiting, diarrhea, nervousness, trembling, lack of coordination, dilation of pupils, muscular weakness, paralysis, coldness of extremities or entire body, weakened and slowed heart-beat, convulsions, and coma. Symptoms begin quickly. Death occurs through respiratory paralysis.

Treatment: Seek immediate medical assistance — a life threatening emergency. Immediately induce vomiting followed by drinking water / vomiting sessions until free of plant material. Give a saline cathartic; administer activated charcoal in water or milk. Preparations should be made to assist respiration (with oxygen if available). If respiration fails, give CPR until medical help arrives.

0 mm	1 cm	2 cm	3 cm	4 cm	5 cm	6 cm	7 cm	8 cm	9 cm	1 dm 10 cm

1 mm = 0.04 inches	1 cm = 0.39 inches	1 dm = 3.94 inches	1 m = 39.37 inches

0 in.	1 in.	2 in.	3 in.	4 in.

Poisonous Plant

Ht: 11 dm

RED ELDERBERRY

Sambucus racemosa (S. pubens) / **CAPRIFOLIACEAE**   **Honeysuckle family**

Other Common Names: Red Elder.

Description: Small shrub to small tree; stems pithy; large pinnately compound leaves, leaf-lets serrate; flowers in a pyramidal or strongly convex panicle-like inflorescence, small, white to cream color; fruit berry-like, usually red but in some varieties black, purplish, or occasionally yellow, chestnut, or white, about 2-3 mm in diameter. This species has several varieties.

Range: Throughout much of North America.

Season: Varies with locality. Flowers in spring; fruit ripens in summer.

Toxic Parts & Toxins: The whole plant is toxic; the root is probably the most poisonous plant part, the flowers and fruit the least. Uncooked berries may cause nausea. The fruit of red berried species is the most toxic. Toxins are an alkaloid and a cyanogenic glycoside, sambunigrin.

Poison Symptoms: Nausea, vomiting, diarrhea, dizziness; in severe cases respiratory failure may occur from cyanide poisoning.

Treatment: Seek immedical medical assistance — a life threatening emergency (cyanide poisoning). Induce vomiting followed by drinking water / vomiting sessions until free of plant material. Give activated charcoal if available.If respiration fails, initiate CPR.

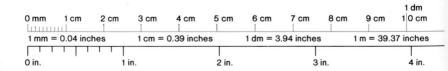

Poisonous Plant

Ht: 5 dm

RHODODENDRON

Rhododendron spp. / **ERICACEAE** **Heath family**

Other Common Names: Rose Bay, Azalea; various species have other, often confusing, common names.

Description: Evergreen or deciduous shrubs varying from small, compact, dwarf forms to small trees; leaves alternate, short stemmed, generally stiff, somewhat brittle and leathery margins entire; flowers in terminal umbel-like racem, rarely in leaf axils or solitary, showy petals forming a saucer, bell, or funnel shaped, five-lobed flower; fruit a capsule.

Range: Cool, moist, and temperate areas. Native species occur along the eastern seaboard in the Appalachian Mountains and in the Pacific Northwest generally west of the Cascades from British Columbia to northern California.

Season: Most species flower in spring; evergreen foliage available throughout the year.

Toxic Parts & Toxins: The leaves, twigs, flowers, pollen, and nectar contain andromedotoxin. Many Ericaceae also contain a glucoside of hydroquinone known as arbutin

Poison Symptoms: Symptoms occur about 6 hours after consumption. Loss of appetite watering of mouth, eyes, and nose, loss of energy, slow pulse, vomiting, diarrhea, low blood pressure, lack of coordination, convulsions, and progressive paralysis of arms and legs until coma and death.

Treatment: Seek medical assistance — a life threatening emergency. Quickly induce vomiting followed by drinking water / vomiting sessions until free of plant material. Vomiting is useful even when several hours have elapsed following consumption. Give activated charcoal if available. If respiratory or circulatory failure occurs, administer CPR.

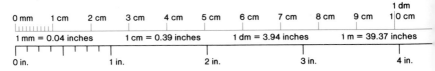

0 mm	1 cm	2 cm	3 cm	4 cm	5 cm	6 cm	7 cm	8 cm	9 cm	1 dm 10 cm

1 mm = 0.04 inches	1 cm = 0.39 inches	1 dm = 3.94 inches	1 m = 39.37 inches

0 in.	1 in.	2 in.	3 in.	4 in.

Poisonous Plant

Ht: 2 m

RHUBARB

Rheum rhaponticum / **POLYGONACEAE** **Buckwheat family**

Other Common Names: Pieplant, Wine Plant.

Description: Stout perennial herb from large fleshy roots with clumps of large heart shaped leaves; leaves with generally long red stalks; leaf blades with entire crinkled margins, often 5 dm or more long; flower stems 1-2 m tall, hollow, branching near top; flower greenish white on slender jointed stalks; fruit a winged seed.

Range: Native to Asia; widely distributed in North America.

Season: Leaves toxic throughout the growing season, however the highest toxic level occurs in late summer and fall.

Toxic Parts & Toxins: The leaf blades contain oxalic acid and oxalates, and are poisonous, both raw and cooked. Oxalate level can vary, but at times small amounts of leaf blade are potentially lethal.

Poison Symptoms: Severe irritation and corrosion of the mouth, stomach, and intestine resulting in nausea, violent vomiting, and bloody diarrhea. Potential kidney failure and urine blockage. Other symptoms include headache, backache, difficulty in breathing, internal bleeding, convulsions, and coma.

Treatment: Seek immediate medical assistance — a life threatening emergency. Fast action is required. Induce vomiting **after** giving milk, lime (the salt) water, chalk, ground calcium tablets. Repeat the procedure. If corrosion of tissue has occurred and medical help is quickly available, do not risk additional tissue damage through the inducement of vomiting

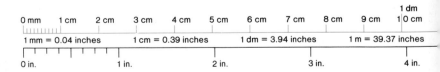

	1 dm
0 mm 1 cm 2 cm 3 cm 4 cm 5 cm 6 cm 7 cm 8 cm 9 cm 10 cm	
1 mm = 0.04 inches 1 cm = 0.39 inches 1 dm = 3.94 inches 1 m = 39.37 inches	

0 in.   1 in.   2 in.   3 in.   4 in.

Poisonous Plant

Ht: 7 dm

SCOTCH BROOM

Cytisus scoparius / **LEGUMINOSAE** **Pea family**

Other Common Names: Scot's Broom.

Description: A bushy, rigidly branched shrub to 3 m tall, branches strongly angled, green; leaves small, trifoliate; flowers pea-like, generally bright yellow but sometimes reddish or purplish, about 2 cm long; fruit a pea-like pod, smooth except for hairy margins, seeds several.

Range: Native to Europe, naturalized along the East Coast from Nova Scotia to Georgia and west of the Cascades from British Columbia to California.

Season: Flowers from April through June; pods follow.

Toxic Parts & Toxins: Most poisoning occurs through the eating of the pod. The plant contains the toxic quinolizidine alkaloids sparteine and isosparteine as well as two minor alkaloids, sarothamnine and genisteine. The plant also contains scoparin.

Poison Symptoms: Information is sparse. Sparteine weakens muscular contractions by paralyzing nerve endings, weakens contractions of the heart resulting in a slow, weak pulse. Breathing becomes labored.

Treatment: Seek medical assistance. Quickly induce vomiting followed by drinking water, vomiting sessions until free of plant material. In severe cases CPR may be necessary.

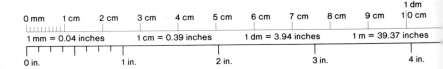

Poisonous Plant

Ht: 7 dm

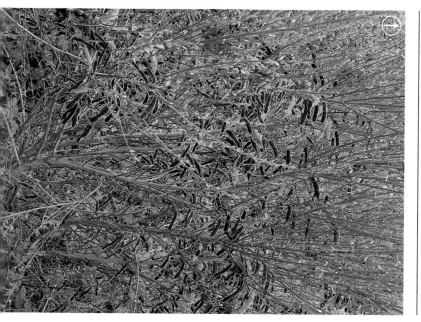

SNOWBERRY

Symphoricarpos albus / **CAPRIFOLIACEAE** **Honeysuckle family**

Other Common Names: Waxberry

Description: Shrubs up to 2 m tall with upright slender branches; leaves round-oval to oblong, 2.5 - 5 cm long, those on young shoots often sinuately lobed; flowers in terminal or axillary spikes or clusters, bell shaped, pinkish; fruit a snow-white berry 6 - 13 mm long.

Range: Nova Scotia to Minnesota and Virginia; Alaska to California and Colorado. Also in cultivation for hedges and ornamental plantings.

Season: Flowers throughout the summer; fruit matures in autumn and persists through winter.

Toxic Parts & Toxins: The fruit reportedly is toxic and the whole plant should be suspect.

Poison Symptoms: Vomiting and drastic catharsis. One case involving children was characterized by delirium followed by a semicomatose state.

Treatment: Administer demulcents (soothing liquid substances) such as milk or egg white if available, prior to inducing vomiting. Follow with additional demulcent. If vomiting and/or diarrhea is extended, particularly in children, great care must be taken to prevent dehydration and electrolyte imbalance. Seek medical assistance.

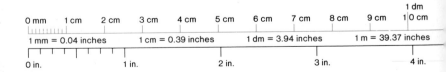

0 mm	1 cm	2 cm	3 cm	4 cm	5 cm	6 cm	7 cm	8 cm	9 cm	1 dm 10 cm

1 mm = 0.04 inches   1 cm = 0.39 inches   1 dm = 3.94 inches   1 m = 39.37 inches

| 0 in. | 1 in. | 2 in. | 3 in. | 4 in. |

SWEET PEA

Lathyrus spp. / **LEGUMINOSAE** **Pea family**

Other Common Names: Wild Pea, Peavine, Vetchling.

Description: Annual or perennial herbs usually with twining stems, stems sometimes winged; leaves pinnately compound, leaflets 2-8 or rarely lacking, tendrils at leaf apex, simple or branched, occasionally reduced to a bristle; flowers pea-like, relatively large and showy, white or yellow to pink, red, or purple; fruit a one-celled pod with several seeds.

Range: Throughout the north temperate zone.

Season: Flowers throughout summer, fruits in summer and fall depending on species and locality.

Toxic Parts & Toxins: The entire plant, especially the seeds (raw or cooked), contain amine-bearing compounds that cause two types of poisoning. One set of species contains L-alpha, gamma-diaminobutyric acid causing internal poisoning, and another set contains beta-(gamma-L-glutamyl)-aminopropionitrile which causes skeletal deformities.

Poison Symptoms: Depending on the species injested, symptoms range from hyperexcitability, convulsions, and death, or possible permanent paralysis, skeletal deformity with growth suppression, and in severe cases death follows. Paralysis is generally confined to the legs but may include the arms and/or extend to loss of bladder and/or bowel control.

Treatment: Seek immediate medical assistance — a life threatening emergency. Induce vomiting followed by drinking water/vomiting sessions until free of plant material. Administer activated charcoal if available. If breathing fails, initiate CPR.

0 mm	1 cm	2 cm	3 cm	4 cm	5 cm	6 cm	7 cm	8 cm	9 cm	1 dm 10 cm

1 mm = 0.04 inches   1 cm = 0.39 inches   1 dm = 3.94 inches   1 m = 39.37 inches

0 in.   1 in.   2 in.   3 in.   4 in.

WATER HEMLOCK

Cicuta douglasii / **UMBELLIFERAE   Parsley family**

Other Common Names: American Cowbane, Fool's Parsley, Poison Hemlock, Water Parsnip, Poison Parsnip, Beaver Poison.

Description: Erect, stout, hollow stemmed, branching perennial; sturdy lower stem 6 dm to 2 m from thick rootstalk(s) containing cavities and cross partitions; leaves alternate, 1-3 times pinnate, leaflets 3-10 cm by 5-35 mm with obvious veins terminating at the serrate notches; flowers borne in flat-topped compound umbels, white to greenish-white, small; fruit 2-4 mm, prominent, longitudinal corky ribs. Cut stalk exudes a yellowish, oily liquid.

Range: Widely distributed throughout the western U.S. and Canada as far north as Alaska in marsh areas, swamps, ditches, and along stream borders.

Season: Flowers in summer; roots toxic throughout year.

Toxic Parts & Toxins: Cicutoxin, an unsaturated aliphatic alcohol, occurs throughout the entire plant. The highest concentration is in the stem and rootstalk, and a single piece 1 cm in diameter can be lethal.

Poison Symptoms: Within 15 minutes to one hour nausea, salivation, vomiting, diarrhea, and tremors, followed quickly by extremely violent intermittent seizures, respiratory failure, and cardiac arrest. Pupils are dilated and temperature may be elevated. Death can occur within 15 minutes.

Treatment: Seek medical assistance — a life threatening emergency. Induce vomiting followed by drinking water / vomiting sessions until free of plant material. Danger of asphyxiation from inhaled vomitus. Give activated charcoal if available. When respiration and/or cardiac failure occur, implement CPR with oxygen if available.

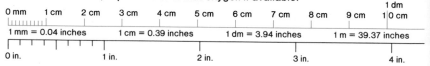

0 mm	1 cm	2 cm	3 cm	4 cm	5 cm	6 cm	7 cm	8 cm	9 cm	1 dm 10 cm

1 mm = 0.04 inches   1 cm = 0.39 inches   1 dm = 3.94 inches   1 m = 39.37 inches

0 in.	1 in.	2 in.	3 in.	4 in.

WILD TOBACCO

Nicotiana attenuata / **SOLANACEAE**   **Nightshade family**

Other Common Names: Coyote Tobacco.

Description: Strongly odorous annual herb, 3-10 dm; leaves entire, the lowermost with stems and lance-ovate to elliptic blades 2.5-12 cm long and 1-5 cm wide, progressively smaller towards the shoot tip; the whole plant glandular-hairy; flowers dirty white with a narrow tube abruptly spreading outward near the top; fruit a capsule.

Range: East of the Cascade Mountains from southern British Columbia to Baja California, Sonora, and Texas.

Season: Flowers from summer to frost depending on locality.

Toxic Parts & Toxins: All parts of the plant are poisonous, containing the extremely poisonous alkaloid, nicotine, as well as other toxic compounds.

Poison Symptoms: Severe vomiting, diarrhea, slow pulse, dizziness, collapse, and respiratory failure.

Treatment: Induce vomiting if it hasn't already occurred, followed by drinking water / vomiting sessions until free of plant material. Administer strong tea and, if available, activated charcoal. If respiratory failure occurs, administer CPR. Seek immediate medical assistance.

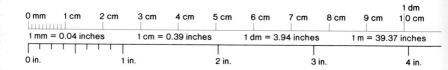

Poisonous Plant

Ht: 6 dm

WISTERIA

Wisteria spp. / **LEGUMINOSAE** **Pea family**

Other Common Names: Japanese, Chinese, and Silky Wisteria.

Description: Woody twiners often reaching great age with trunks 1 dm or more in diameter; leaves pinnately compound with 9-19 leaflets; flowers pea-like, blue, purple, lilac, or white in long drooping racemes; fruit a flattened many seeded pod, velvety hairy in the commonly cultivated species but glabrous in wild species of the southeastern and southern U.S.

Range: Native species occur from Virginia to southern Missouri, south to Florida and Texas. The Asian species are widely cultivated, especially in mild climates, and can be expected around houses, old farmsteads, etc. in all except the most northern areas of the U.S.

Season: Flowers in late spring and early summer; pods follow.

Toxic Parts & Toxins: All parts, especially seeds and seed pods, are poisonous. One or two seeds are said to be enough to cause serious illness. Toxins are poorly characterized; sapotoxins, resin, and a glucoside have been reported.

Poison Symptoms: Mild to severe gastroenteritis with repeated vomiting, diarrhea (usually slight), and abdominal pain, dehydration. Although patients sometimes are put on the critical list due to severity of symptoms, recovery is generally complete in 24 to 48 hours.

Treatment: Quickly induce vomiting if this has not already occurred. Follow with drinking water / vomiting sessions until free of plant material. Give activated charcoal if available. Give clear liquids to counteract dehydration.

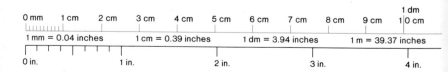

| 0 mm | 1 cm | 2 cm | 3 cm | 4 cm | 5 cm | 6 cm | 7 cm | 8 cm | 9 cm | 1 dm 10 cm |

1 mm = 0.04 inches   1 cm = 0.39 inches   1 dm = 3.94 inches   1 m = 39.37 inches

| 0 in. | 1 in. | 2 in. | 3 in. | 4 in. |

Poisonous Plant

Ht: 5 m

WOODY NIGHTSHADE

Solanum dulcamara / **SOLANACEAE   Nightshade family**

Other Common Names: Bittersweet, Scarlet Berry, Violet Bloom, Deadly Nightshade, Climbing Nightshade.

Description: Shrub-like perennial from woody base with slender trailing branches to 4-(8)m, especially when supported by hedges, bushes, and fences; leaves are alternate, ovate with opposing lobes at base; leaves and stems have distinctive unpleasant odor; flower is bluish purple, sometimes white, 1-2 cm across, loosely clustered, hanging from leaf axil; berries oval, green when unripe, bright red when mature, to 10 mm diameter.

Range: Native to Eurasia; found in moist rich soil in forests, thickets, and waste places throughout North America with most frequent distribution in northern United States.

Season: Both blossoms and berries at any state of maturity are apt to be found on the same plant throughout the summer into late autumn. Berries can remain on plant after leaves have fallen.

Toxic Parts & Toxins: Solanine and other glycoalkaloids are found throughout the plant with greatest concentration in unripe fruit.

Poison Symptoms: Nervousness, abdominal pain, vomiting, diarrhea, shock, circulatory and respiratory depression, below normal temperature, pupil dilation, paralysis, loss of sensation, and death.

Treatment: Seek immediate medical assistance — a life threatening emergency. Quickly induce vomiting. Administer drinking water / vomiting sessions until vomit is free of plant material. Cardiac symptoms usually occur within 2-4 hours with maximum effect in about 8-10 hours. Some symptoms may persist for two to three weeks.

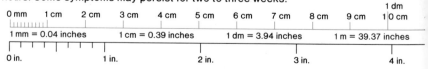

0 mm	1 cm	2 cm	3 cm	4 cm	5 cm	6 cm	7 cm	8 cm	9 cm	1 dm 10 cm

1 mm = 0.04 inches   1 cm = 0.39 inches   1 dm = 3.94 inches   1 m = 39.37 inches

0 in.	1 in.	2 in.	3 in.	4 in.

Ht: 4 m

YELLOW JESSAMINE

Gelsemium sempervirens / **LOGANIACEAE** **Logania family**

Other Common Names: False Jasmine, Wild Woodbine, Evening Trumpetflower.

Description: Woody, twining stemmed, climbing evergreen vine with primary stem grey-colored, to 25 mm diameter and up to 5 m or more with support; younger stems many-branched, tangled, shiny red-brown; leaves lanceolate, opposite, about 4-7 cm long; 1-5 large funnel-shaped, fragrant yellow flowers from axillary clusters; two long fruit (seeds) contained in jointed pods, numerous, flat winged.

Range: East Coastal Plain from Virginia south to Florida and extending west to Tennessee, Arkansas and Texas, and into Mexico in rich, moist soils, along stream borders and fencerows.

Season: Flowers in late winter or early spring.

Toxic Parts & Toxins: All parts of the plant contain the alkaloids gelsemine, gelseminine and gelsemoidine with the greatest concentration in roots and flower nectar.

Poison Symptoms: Depression, heavy perspiration, muscular weakness and/or rigidity, respiratory depression, convulsions, and paralysis of motor nerve endings. Headache, dizziness, dimness of vision. Death is through respiratory failure.

Treatment: Seek immediate medical assistance — a life threatening emergency. Quickly induce vomiting. Administer drinking water/vomiting sessions until vomit is free of plant material. Cardiac symptoms usually occur within 2-4 hours with maximum effect in about 8-10 hours. Some symptoms may persist for two to three weeks.

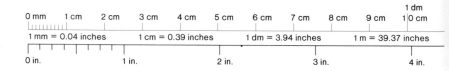

Poisonous Plant

Ht: 3 m

YEW

Taxus spp. / **TAXACEAE   Yew family**

Other Common Names: T. canadensis sometimes called Ground Hemlock.

Description: Low growing shrubs to trees; bark scaly, reddish-brown; branchlets irregularly alternate on main branches; leaves (needles) generally 2-ranked, yellowish beneath and without resin ducts, leaf bases appearing to extend down branchlet; male cones minute, shed pollen in spring, but female develops into a seed surrounded by a red, fleshy aril or "berry."

Range: Native species occur in the Pacific Northwest and in the Northwest and Midwest. Yew is also widely planted as an ornamental.

Season: The needles are evergreen and available throughout the year. Arils develop in summer and persist into winter.

Toxic Parts & Toxins: All parts of the plant except the fleshy aril that surrounds the seed are poisonous. At least 10 alkaloids are known; the most important are taxine A and B.

Poison Symptoms: Appear quickly, usually within a hour, and include dizziness, dry throat, marked dilatation of the pupils, colic and vomiting, muscular weakness, and stupor followed by loss of consciousness. Other symptoms can include red spots on the skin, facial pallor, and purple discoloration of lips. Toxine is depressant causing the heart heat to become slow, irregular, and then stop.

Treatment: Seek immediate medical assistance — a life threatening emergency. Quick action is extremely important. Immediately induce vomiting followed by drinking water vomiting sessions until free of plant material. In serious cases CPR may be required.

0 mm	1 cm	2 cm	3 cm	4 cm	5 cm	6 cm	7 cm	8 cm	9 cm	1 dm 10 cm

1 mm = 0.04 inches	1 cm = 0.39 inches	1 dm = 3.94 inches	1 m = 39.37 inches

0 in.	1 in.	2 in.	3 in.	4 in.

Poisonous Plant

Ht: 2 m

POISONOUS PLANTS
(Causing Contact Poisoning)

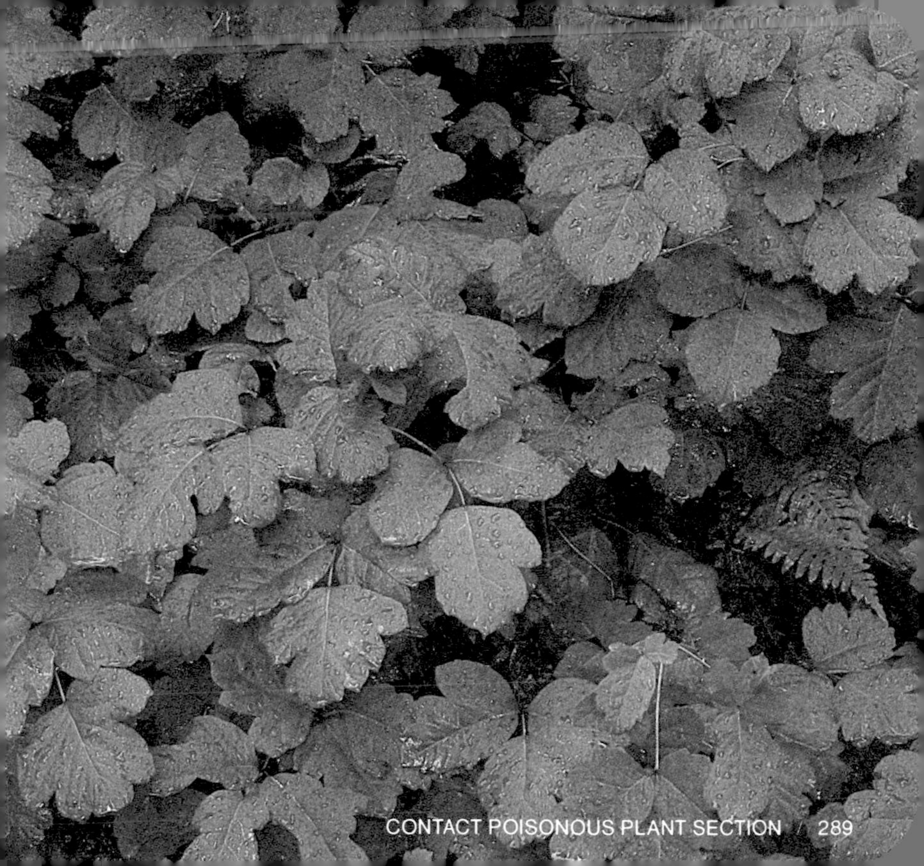

COW PARSNIP

Heracleum lanatum / **UMBELLIFERAE**   **Parsley family**

Other Common Names: Wild Parsnip, Wild Rhubarb

Description: Single-stemmed perennial 1-3 m tall; leaves once ternate with broad, distinctly stalked, coarsely toothed, and palmately lobed leaflets; leaflets 1-4 dm long and wide; stems and leaves usually with hairs; flowers white, borne in compound umbels, the terminal umbel 1-2 dm wide; fruit obovate to obcordate, 7-12 mm long x 5-9 mm wide. Crushed tissue has aromatic, somewhat unpleasant, parsnip-like odor.

Range: Widespread in North America.

Season: Flowers in early summer.

Toxic Parts & Toxins: The sap contains furocomarins (psoralens) that produce a phototoxic reaction that makes the skin hypersensitive to sunlight.

Poison Symptoms: Poison Ivy-like eruptions on the skin after contact with the sap and subsequent exposure to sunlight. Scarring and brown discoloration of the skin may last for years. Exposure of lips, eyes, and other sensitive areas is especially dangerous.

Treatment: Treatment should be simple, safe, and conservative as contact dermatitis is usually self-limiting once exposure to the toxic material is eliminated. Cool compresses of plain sterile water applied to the area at half hour intervals are of great help during the acute stages. Exposure to direct sunlight should be avoided. If dermatitis is severe or signs of infection occur, seek medical attention.

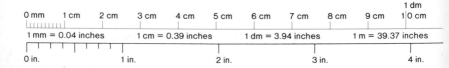

Poisonous Plant

Ht: 12 dm

NETTLE

Urtica dioica / **URTICACEAE   Nettle family**

Other Common Names: Stinging Nettle.

Description: *Uritca:* Annual or perennial herb 1 dm to 5 m tall, armed with stinging hairs; leaves opposite and sharply toothed; flowers very small in dense, frequently drooping clusters. *Urtica dioica:* Perennial herb 7 dm to 3 m tall; creeping rootstalk; leaves are roughly heart-shaped at base, 4-8 cm broad; stems and leaves covered with stinging hairs; green flowers are in slender drooping spikes at leaf-axils.

Range: Widely distributed throughout the U.S. and Canada; frequently in rich, moist, shaded areas. *Urtica dioica* var. *lyallii,* shown here, is common from Alaska to California east to western Montana.

Season: Early spring until late fall.

Toxic Parts & Toxins: Stems and leaves are covered by very sharp stinging hairs which contain an irritating fluid.

Poison Symptoms: The sting hairs pierce the skin, and the venom is instantly released causing temporary inflammation and irritation.

Treatment: Nettle stings are not life threatening. Treatment should be simple, safe, and conservative as the stinging and swelling generally subside in several hours. Folk remedies include rubbing the affected area with dock, rosemary, mint, or sage, but it is unlikely that this has much effect.

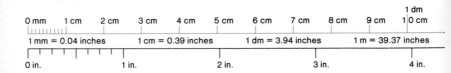

| 0 mm | 1 cm | 2 cm | 3 cm | 4 cm | 5 cm | 6 cm | 7 cm | 8 cm | 9 cm | 1 dm 1 0 cm |

1 mm = 0.04 inches   1 cm = 0.39 inches   1 dm = 3.94 inches   1 m = 39.37 inches

| 0 in. | 1 in. | 2 in. | 3 in. | 4 in. |

Poisonous Plant

Ht: 7 dm

POISON IVY

Rhus radicans, (= Toxicodendron), R. diversiloba / **ANACARDIACEAE**   **Sumac family**

Other Common Names: Poison Oak.

Description: Shrubs or woody vines to 2 m tall and vining to 15 m; leaves with 3 glossy leaflets, usually turning bright red in the fall; flowers small, greenish-white, clustered in the leaf axils; fruits berry-like, white, waxy, 4-5 mm in diameter.

Range: Throughout most of North America, east of the Cascade Mountains, Great Basin, and Mojave Desert.

Season: Plants dangerous throughout the year, fruit ripens in August through November and persists all winter.

Toxic Parts & Toxins: There are four closely related toxins, including urushiol (3-n-pentadecylcatechol), contained in resin canals throughout the plant. The poison may also be spread by smoke from burning the plant material.

Poison Symptoms: Dermatitis with reddened itchy skin in mild cases to blisters which exude serum in the most severe cases. Death may result from ingestion of leaves or fruit. Combination of the poison with skin proteins is thought to occur immediately on contact. Death can occur in very severe cases.

Treatment: Washing with strong soap apparently serves only to remove excess poison which might be spread to other parts of the body, but it is a useful first aid step that should be done as quickly as possible although it won't eliminate reactions in sensitive people. Treatment is only symptomatic; there is no known cure. Give starch or oatmeal baths to treat itching. If urinary output is normal, give 2-4 liters of fluid daily. Launder clothing and expose to air and sunlight for 48 hours. In severe cases seek medical attention.

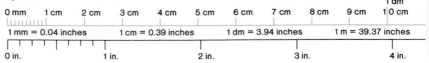

| 0 mm | 1 cm | 2 cm | 3 cm | 4 cm | 5 cm | 6 cm | 7 cm | 8 cm | 9 cm | 1 dm 10 cm |

1 mm = 0.04 inches   1 cm = 0.39 inches   1 dm = 3.94 inches   1 m = 39.37 inches

0 in.   1 in.   2 in.   3 in.   4 in.

Poisonous Plant

Ht: 4 dm

POISON OAK

Rhus diversiloba (= Toxicodendron diversilobum), R. radicans /
ANACARDIACEAE   Sumac family

Other Common Names: Poison Oak.

Description: Shrubs or woody vines to 2 m tall and vining to 15 m; leaves with 3 glossy leaflets, usually turning bright red in the fall; flowers small, greenish-white, clustered in the leaf axils; fruits berry-like, white, waxy, 4-5 mm in diameter.

Range: Throughout most of temperate North America. From southern British Columbia to northern Baja. between Cascades and Coast Ranges in Washington and Oregon, and west of Sierra Nevada Mountains and Mojave Desert in California.

Season: Plants dangerous throughout the year.

Toxic Parts & Toxins: Presumably the same as for *R. radicans* (Poison Ivy), contained in resin canals throughout the plant. The poison may also be spread by smoke from burning the plant material.

Poison Symptoms: Dermatitis with reddened itchy skin in mild cases to blisters which exude serum in the most severe cases. Death may result from ingestion of leaves or fruit. Combination of the poison with skin proteins is thought to occur immediately on contact. Death can occur in very severe cases.

Treatment: Washing with strong soap apparently serves only to remove excess poison which might be spread to other parts of the body, but it is a useful first aid step that should be done as quickly as possible, although it won't eliminate reactions in sensitive people. Treatment is only symptomatic; there is no known cure. Give starch or oatmeal baths to treat itching. If urinary output is normal, give 2-4 liters of fluid daily. Launder clothing and expose to air and sunlight for 48 hours. In severe cases seek medical attention.

0 mm	1 cm	2 cm	3 cm	4 cm	5 cm	6 cm	7 cm	8 cm	9 cm	1 dm 10 cm

1 mm = 0.04 inches	1 cm = 0.39 inches	1 dm = 3.94 inches	1 m = 39.37 inches

0 in.	1 in.	2 in.	3 in.	4 in.

Poisonous Plant

Ht: 5 dm

Rhus diversiloba **Sumac Family**

Rhus diversiloba / 297

POISON SUMAC

Rhus vernix (= Toxicodendron vernix) / **ANACARDIACEAE**   **Sumac family**

Other Common Names: Poison Elder.

Description: Coarse shrub 2-7 m tall; gray bark; leaves odd-pinnately compound, 7-13 leaflets; leaflets ascending, oblong-ovate to ovate-lanceolate, margins entire (nonpoisonous sumacs toothed); flowers small, greenish-white to cream color, abundant, in axillary panicles up to 2 dm long; glossy, pale yellow, cream, or drab white, globular.

Range: Southern Quebec and Maine to central Florida and east Texas, generally east of the Mississippi River, but known from neighboring states to the west. Found in bogs, swamps, and wet bottom lands. (Non-toxic sumacs rarely occur in these wet habitats.)

Season: Plants dangerous throughout the year. Flowers in May through July.

Toxic Parts & Toxins: The entire plant is dangerous. The toxins are similar to those found in *Rhus radicans* (Poison Ivy).

Poison Symptoms: Dermatitis with reddened itchy skin in mild cases to blisters which exude serum in the most severe cases. Death may result from ingestion of leaves or fruit. Combination of the poison with skin proteins is thought to occur immediately on contact. Death can occur in very severe cases.

Treatment: Washing with strong soap apparently serves only to remove excess poison which might be spread to other parts of the body, but it is a useful first aid step that should be done as quickly as possible although it won't eliminate reactions in sensitive people. Treatment is only symptomatic; there is no known cure. Give starch or oatmeal baths to treat itching. If urinary output is normal, give 2-4 liters of fluid daily. Launder clothing and expose to air and sunlight for 48 hours. In severe cases seek medical attention.

0 mm	1 cm	2 cm	3 cm	4 cm	5 cm	6 cm	7 cm	8 cm	9 cm	1 dm / 10 cm

1 mm = 0.04 inches   1 cm = 0.39 inches   1 dm = 3.94 inches   1 m = 39.37 inches

0 in.		1 in.		2 in.		3 in.		4 in.

Poisonous Plant

Ht: 2 m

FIRST AID

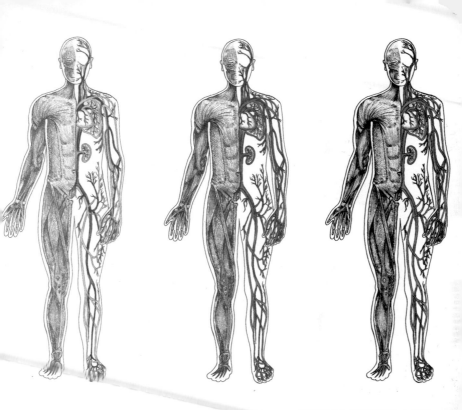

INTRODUCTION

Illness and injury are always potential survival partners. **Nature Bound** is intended to provide information which will first, ideally, prevent the necessity of the implementation of first aid procedures. However, because "ideal" is not normally the circumstance of a survivalist, we are compelled to discuss first aid as it relates to the wilderness experience with the objective of minimizing and controlling illness and injury in the field.

We have divided this section into two primary topics. The first deals with survival health and hygiene. The second covers first aid procedures for a number of the more common injuries and maladies related to the backcountry. This section covers the definition, cause, symptoms, and treatment for each condition discussed.

Understanding that **you** are apt to become the "field doctor" for either yourself or others carries with it a substantial responsibility. A thorough understanding of this will not wait for the inconvenience of a field emergency. The subject is one for which there is a good amount of low or no cost instruction. The American Red Cross, American Heart Association, local rescue and fire departments, Public Health Service, and your family doctor are all excellent sources providing information which will be of value both at home and in the field. The simple fact that such training and information could save a life (maybe even your own) should be all the incentive you need to attend a series on first aid or to take a four hour CPR (cardiopulmonary resuscitation) course. As with insurance, there is a correlation between investment and benefit.

The first rule of medicine is: **Do no harm.** Do not attempt to treat beyond your skill or training. The primary concern in most life threatening injuries is to stabilize the patient's condition and provide the necessary care to prevent complication. Once this has been reasonably dealt with, obtaining medical assistance becomes the next priority.

And now, enjoy the asurance that your training, knowledge, and this pocket field guide will provide you with the credentials to deal with most wilderness emergencies — and that these will make your wilderness stay enjoyable if planned, tolerable if unplanned.

STP LIFE SAVING PROCEDURES

In treating the injured person, you should follow what is known as the STP Life Saving Procedures.

1. STOP the bleeding. Apply direct pressure on the wound.
2. TREAT shock. Keep patient warm and quiet.
3. PROTECT the injury. Bandage to guard against infection.

Injuries such as cuts, bruises, fractures, sprains, concussions, and burns typify those most frequently encountered in the outdoors. In case of a severe injury, keep the patient lying down. If the patient is unconscious, keep him lying on his stomach with his head turned to the side to prevent choking — unless the neck or head is injured. In this case lie him on his back and elevate the head — unless a broken neck is suspected. (It should be noted that in 15% of the cases where a head injury has led to unconsciousness, a neck fracture exists.)

Handle the patient carefully, especially if a fracture or back injury is suspected. Patients with a back or neck injury should be moved only when absolutely essential.

Try to keep all improvised equipment sterile. Improvised bandages and dressings can be sufficiently sterilized by boiling or steaming in a covered container, or even charred if water is unavailable. Intense heat is an adequate method for sterilizing most other equipment used in treating the injured.

I. SURVIVAL HEALTH & HYGIENE

Prevention is the suitable alternative to first aid. So, before describing technique for dealing with the emergency medical situations which may arise in the course of a wilderness stay, practices of preventing some of these emergency situations should be discussed. Many potentially harmful predicaments can be avoided by the sustained practices of good diet, cleanliness, and the use of appropriate clothing; and others can be reduced to matters of routine, provided one has the knowledge of how to proceed safely.

Many diseases, as well as infection, sustained bleeding, and even the frequency of some insect bites can be avoided, or at least mollified, by perpetuating a good diet. Consult some of the many nutrition books or a doctor in order to establish a healthy diet. While often it is possible to continue a fairly adequate diet under survival conditions, remember that it often requires several weeks for the full effect of slight changes in diet to become evident in the body. The body which enters the woods the healthiest is the most likely to exit alive.

Clothing is the other side of cleanliness. Besides the body, the one thing usually carried into a survival situation is the clothing worn at the time. Clothing too brief or too heavy can result in fatal loss of water through perspiration. Clothing too light can invite fatal loss of body heat. Inadequate footwear can result in breaks, sprains, and blisters. Take the time to determine what sort of clothing is required by the area and season of travel.

The survivalist's overall physical and mental condition by and large effectively controls his morale, ability to function, and will to live. Furthermore, the physical and mental states are primarily the functions of good health and proper hygiene. Keeping clean and well, therefore, is especially important when you are on your own.

As a practical matter, protecting yourself from disease and infection involves making personal habits of a number of simple rules which we will call personal survival hygiene.

1. **Keep Clean**
   a. Body cleanliness is the first defense against disease germs. A daily shower with hot water and soap is ideal but generally not feasible in the survival situation. Do keep the hands as clean as possible and sponge the face, armpits, crotch, and feet at least once a day.
   b. Keep your clothing, especially your underclothing and socks, as clean as possible. If laundering is impossible, shake out your clothing and expose to sun and air daily.
   c. If you have a toothbrush, use it regularly. Table salt and soda make good substitutes for toothpaste. Even mashed aspirin will work. If a toothbrush is unavailable, an improvised one can be made by chewing the end of a small green twig into a pulpy consistency. After eating, rinse the mouth — if purified water is available.
2. **Guard Against Intestinal Sickness.** Common diarrhea, food poisoning, and other intestinal disorders are the commonest, if not the most serious, of the diseases you will have to guard against. They are caused by putting filth or poisons into the mouth and stomach. The following rules of hygiene can normally prevent these maladies.
   a. Keep the body, particularly the hands, clean. Keep the fingers away from the mouth. Avoid handling food with the hands except as is necessary.
   b. Purify your drinking water by use of purification tablets or by boiling for at least four minutes — 10-15 minutes if there is a possibility that the water is contaminated by the organism, Giardia lamblia (an organism which causes Giardiasis, "beaver fever," an infection within the small intestine resulting in diarrhea, vomiting and nausea). The probability of the presence of this organism increases where beavers are present. Sheep and dogs are also suspected carriers of this organism which enters the water through animal feces. Remoteness does not insure the absence of this organism, although it is less likely nearer water's source.
   c. Avoid eating raw foods, especially those grown on or in the ground.
   d. Avoid holding food for long periods following preparation.

e. Sterilize your eating utensils with heat.
f. Keep flies and other vermin off your food and drink.
g. Keep your camp area and shelter clean.
h. Adopt strict measures for disposing of human waste and garbage.

3. **Guard Against Heat Injury.** In hot climates develop a tan by gradual exposure to the sun. Avoid strenuous exertion in the hot sun; it can lead to fatal heat stroke. The lesser illnesses caused by heat (heat cramps and heat exhaustion) can be prevented by consuming enough water and salt to replace the sweat.

4. **Guard Against Cold Injury.** When exposed to severe cold, conserve your body heat by every means possible. Take particular care of your feet, hands, and exposed parts. Keep your socks dry and use any available material, including rags and paper, to improvise protective covering. Frostbite is a constant danger to anyone exposed to temperatures below freezing (usually below 10° F.). Tight constricting clothing and foot gear can retard circulation. This, combined with the normal body reaction to cold (the body decreases blood flow to superficial tissues to prevent excessive heat loss), is apt to retard adequate blood flow to maintain tissue health.

5. **Guard Against Insects and Insect-born Diseases.** Common insects such as flies, mosquitoes, lice, ticks, and mites carry many of our most serious diseases.

6. **Take care of the Feet**
    a. Do not wear dirty or sweaty socks. If a clean pair is not available, wash out the pair being worn. If you have an extra pair to wear, put the washed pair inside your shirt next to your body to dry. Wool socks are best in that they can absorb a fair amount of foot perspiration without causing problems to the feet.
    b. Blisters are dangerous in that they can lead to infections. If the shoes fit well and clean sock recommendations are followed, you should have little problem with blisters. Of course, wet shoes should be dried.

II. FIRST AID

1. **Bleeding**
    a. Place sterile dressing or clean substitute (sock, T-shirt, etc.) directly on the wound, applying hand pressure. Then bandage the wound firmly.
    b. If the bleeding is from an arm or leg, and if the bleeding continues, elevate the injured limb and continue the pressure. 98% of all bleeding can be controlled in this manner.
    c. If the bleeding continues in spite of pressure dressing and elevation of the injured area, a tourniquet may be required.
    d. Tourniquet — **the last resort**.
       What is?
       A band of constriction placed around a limb and shutting off the blood supply to points beyond.
       When use?
       Only when there is partial or complete amputation of the limb or in cases of severe, uncontrollable bleeding. In short, a tourniquet is a **last resort** measure against life-threatening bleeding.
       Where place?
       Apply it between the wound and the heart. In cases of traumatic amputation (loss of arm, leg, hand, or foot), place tourniquet near end of the stump above unbroken skin. In all other cases where a tourniquet is required to control bleeding, place it above elbow or knee. Once applied, do not loosen or remove.
2. **Lacerations (Cuts)**
    a. Definition:
       A cut or tear in the skin surface in which the degree of seriousness is measured by the location on the body and the size, shape, and depth of the injury. Fortunately, most lacerations in the field are shallow and occur on the extremities with the control of external bleeding the primary concern.

b. Symptoms:
   Obvious, generally accompanied by bleeding.
c. Treatment:
   (1) Minor lacerations
       (a) Control the bleeding by using a pressure bandage.
       (b) Clean the wound and area around the wound. Wash thoroughly with mild soap if available. Remove foreign material (dirt, slivers, glass, etc.).
       (c) If the laceration is located on a body part where fatty tissue protrudes through the wound opening (common in chin lacerations) or the wound opening is inclined to stretch or stay spread, dry the skin on both sides of the wound and apply a "butterfly" bandage or sterile paper tape (steristrips) if available. Apply in a manner that brings the edges of the wound together without rolling or folding under, being careful not to trap bits of the fatty tissue between the edges.
       (d) Apply an antibacterial ointment and a sterile dressing.
   (2) Major lacerations
       (a) Control the bleeding by using a pressure bandage.
       (b) Evaluate the seriousness of the injury. Is a fracture involved? Carefully check for tendon, nerve, or major arterial damage. This can be done quickly by feeling pulses distal (farther from the heart) to the cut, testing flexion or extension (movement in all directions) of all joints near the cut, and testing for sensation around and distal to the cut.
       (c) Clean the wound area thoroughly using a mild soap. Remove any foreign material.
       (d) When extensive damage to bone, nerves, blood vessels exists, apply a protective dressing and
       (e) If a fracture of a limb or appendage is involved, immobilization through splinting should follow. (See 4. Fractures.)
       (f) Obtain medical assistance.

3. Shock
a. Definition:
A disturbance in the equilibrium wherein the normal mental and emotional faculties are impaired or impeded.
b. Cause:
Shock is caused by bodily reaction, usually to an injury or other traumatic event, which slows or stops the circulatory function restricting the flow of blood and oxygen to vital organs.
c. Symptoms:
(1) Weakness, paleness, trembling, sweating, and thirstiness.
(2) Pulse becomes rapid and weak.
(3) Victim may gasp for air — even pass out.
(4) The more severe the injury, the more likely shock will occur.
(5) Shock can, and often does, result in death if not treated.
d. Treatment:
(1) Handle the patient gently and only when necessary.
(2) Remove any bulky items (i.e. packs, etc.).
(3) Loosen belt and clothing.
(4) If conscious, place patient on back.
(5) If unconscious, place face down, head to one side.
(6) Except in the case of a head injury or suspected neck fracture, lower head and shoulders and elevate feet approximately 15 inches so as to increase flow of blood to the brain.
(7) Make sure that there are no broken bones before straightening the patient out.
(8) Protect the patient from becoming chilled or cold. Provide protection from the ground cold as well as an over cover. The important thing here is to keep the patient comfortably warm.
(9) If conscious, not vomiting, and no abdominal injury exists, allow the patient to sip warm drinks.
(10) Continue to reassure the patient.

(11) If you are alone, follow the above as much as possible; if circumstances permit, allow patient to rest for 24 hours.
e. Prevention:
Although there is no positive prevention for shock, it is possible in some instances to prevent it by treating for it. This applies whether or not symptoms are present.

4. Fractures
a. Definitions:
(1) Simple fracture: A break or crack in the bone which does not puncture or penetrate the skin and may not be obvious.
(2) Compound fracture: A break in the bone whereby the skin is broken by the protruding bone, or an open wound in the area of a fracture.
b. Cause:
A fracture normally occurs when the pressure of a blow to or the wrenching of a body part exceeds the bone's ability to absorb that pressure.
c. Symptoms:
(1) Victim unable to move injured part.
(2) Injured part appears deformed.
(3) Pain when attempting to move the part.
(4) Absence of feeling when touched.
(5) Bluish color in injured area.
(6) Swelling.
d. Treatment:
(1) Do not move the victim unless necessary for safety.
(2) If the fracture is accompanied by a wound, tear or cut away the clothing and treat the wound before splinting.
(3) Splint the patient before moving him. Improvise pieces of equipment. Pad the splint and place so that it supports the joints above and below the fracture. Immobilize a fractured leg by tying it to the unbroken leg if no other materials are available. Elevate.

e. Prevention:
    Minimize the potential by exercising reasonable care, particularly in those activities which require above normal physical exertion and risk.

5. Sprains
a. Definition:
    A sudden or violent twist or wrench of a joint.
b. Cause:
    A sprain results when the ligaments which hold together the bones at the joints are wrenched or torn.
c. Symptoms:
    (1) Pain or tenderness in joint (also above and below).
    (2) Generally rapid swelling of area.
    (3) Frequently black and blue skin discoloration occurs.
    (4) Because the symptoms are similar to a fracture, it may be difficult to determine which the patient has. Treat as a fracture if there is any doubt.
d. Treatment:
    (1) Bandage and elevate the sprained limb.
    (2) Apply cold applications for the first 24 hours after the injury, then apply heat.
    (3) If it is absolutely necessary to use the sprained limb, splint or bind the injured area before attempting to use it. Normally the amount of pain will dictate to what extent use is possible.
e. Prevention:
    The potential for the most common sprain, that of the ankle, can be effectively minimized by wearing proper foot gear. Keep in mind that many sprains occur as a result of poor judgment (sliding down hills or embankments, jumping rather than climbing over obstacles, running downhill, etc.). A walking or hiking stick is also a good deterrent to this type of injury. A sprain can be a most debilitating and painful injury which involves an especial inconvenience in the bush.

6. Head Injuries and Concussion

  a. Definition:

    A head wound may consist of one or more of the following conditions:

    (1) A cut or bruise of the scalp.

    (2) A fracture of the skull.

    (3) An injury of the blood vessels of the scalp, skull, and brain.

    (4) An injury to the brain.

    Frequently, serious skull fractures and brain injuries occur together.

  b. Cause:

    Most head injuries in the wilderness are the result of a fall of some type or of being struck in the head (limb, rock, etc.).

  c. Symptoms:

    Suspect a brain injury if the individual:

    (1) Is or has recently been unconscious.

    (2) Has blood or other fluid escaping from the nose or ears.

    (3) Has a headache.

    (4) Has a slow pulse.

    (5) Is vomiting.

    (6) Has had a convulsion.

    (7) Has different-sized eye pupils.

  d. Treatment:

    (1) Keep the patient warm and dry and handle him gently.

    (2) Restrict fluid intake during the first 24 hours.

    (3) Control high temperature with sponge bath of water and cold packs.

    (4) Give no medication by mouth (i.e. aspirin).

    (5) Patient should be closely watched until medical help arrives.

    (6) Keep the patient lying down and treat for shock.

    (7) Elevate head and shoulders slightly if face is flushed.

    (8) Do not elevate head if face appears deadly pale in color.

    (9) To control bleeding from head place a gauze compress lightly over injury, being careful not to apply pressure on injured area.

   e. Prevention:
     Using good judgment on the trail, especially when rock climbing, effectively minimizes the chance of head injuries. Special precautions are also necessary when using an ax.

7. Burns
   a. Definition:
     There are three burn classifications:
     (1) First degree burn: characterized by reddened skin.
     (2) Second degree burn: characterized by blisters.
     (3) Third degree burn: destruction of tissue and underlying cells.
   b. Cause:
     Most burns in the wilderness are of the first and second degree class and result from carelessness around the camp fire.
   c. Symptoms:
     Covered in definition (7a).
   d. Treatment:
     (1) First degree burns should be dealt with by immersing in cold or cool water, cleansing with mild white soap, and bandaging if necessary.
     (2) Second degree burns, when covering only a small area of skin and when the skin is unbroken, can be immersed in cool water. However, no effort to cleanse the burn should be made so as to avoid breaking the blisters. Cover loosely with a bandage to keep the air away. Treat patient for shock.
     (3) Major second degree and third degree burns are almost impossible to treat in the field. Wrap the patient carefully, treat for shock, provide liquid only to the extent it does not cause nausea, and get help.
   e. Prevention:
     Safe practices when building a fire, cooking, and securing the fire for night will substantially eliminate the possibility of camp fire related burns.

8. Intestinal Illness (Diarrhea)
   a. Definition:
     Abnormally frequent intestinal evacuations with more or less fluid stools.

b. Cause:
Generally the result of an infection of the intestinal tract caused by putting filth in the mouth, eating spoiled food, or drinking polluted water. Nervousness and anxiety can also precipitate diarrhea.

c. Symptoms:
   (1) Frequent soft or watery stools.
   (2) Abdominal cramping.
   (3) Feeling of urgency.
   (4) Vomiting.
   (5) Nausea.

d. Treatment:
   (1) Without the availability of a paregoric, field treatment is limited.
   (2) Rest and fast, except for water, for about 24 hours.
   (3) After 24 hours take only liquid foods avoiding sugars and starches. Continue this diet until all symptoms cease.

e. Prevention:
Adequate care in camp sanitation, personal hygiene, and food handling will substantially reduce the possibility of this malady.

9. Heat Injury (Heatstroke, Sunstroke)
a. Definition:
Extremely serious reaction to prolonged exposure to high temperature. The heat-regulating mechanisms in the brain are paralyzed.

b. Cause:
Prolonged exposure to high temperature.

c. Symptoms:
   (1) Hot and dry skin, absence of perspiration.
   (2) Body temperature is high (104 to 110° F.).
   (3) Rapid breathing.
   (4) Dizziness, weakness, nausea, and unconsciousness.
   (5) Symptoms can appear rapidly.

d. Treatment:
  (1) Place victim in shaded area.
  (2) Cool rapidly by whatever means available. Get the victim into a stream or cold lake water. If snow or ice is available, pack about the body in any way possible. Saturate clothing with cold water and fan. Keep cold cloths on head and resoak frequently.
  (3) Continue procedures until temperature drops to 102° or below.
  (4) Get medical assistance.
e. Prevention:
  Avoid prolonged exposure to high temperatures, especially in direct sunlight or while performing strenuous tasks.

10. Cold Injury (Frostbite)

a. Definition:
  The freezing or the local effect of a partial freezing of some part of the body.
b. Cause:
  Exposure, not necessarily prolonged, to subfreezing temperatures (usually below 10° F.). Refer to Wind Chill Chart, 21.1.
c. Symptoms:
  (1) Discoloration of skin (chalky white, yellow-gray, or gray).
  (2) Body part becomes numb and insensitive.
  (3) Extremities and face most susceptible.
d. Treatment:
  (1) Immerse frostbitten part in moderately hot water (105° to 110°).
  .(2) Continue treatment until area has softened.
  (3) Do not rub affected area with hands or with oils, snow, or ice.
  (4) Do not force off frozen shoes or mittens.
  (5) Do not exercise frozen area.
  (6) If sheltered area unavailable, thaw frozen part by using body heat as warming source (frozen hand under armpit, between thighs, etc.).
  (7) Do not thaw the frozen part (especially the toes or feet) if there is a chance they may refreeze before the victim can obtain medical assistance.

e. Prevention:
   Adequate and proper fitting clothing for the conditions, taking special care in protecting those areas which are most susceptible. Understand the temperature and wind chill relationships.

11. Hypothermia
a. Definition:
   Subnormal temperature of the body.
b. Cause:
   Loss of body heat due to exposure to wind, wet, and cold of not necessarily freezing temperatures.
c. Symptoms:
   (1) Shivering of muscles, developing rigidity of muscles, fatigue, and numbness.
   (2) Lack of coordination and slowing in movement and speech.
   (3) Impairment or loss of awareness, memory, and rationality.
   (4) Extremities swell, often turning blue.
   (5) Pupils of the eyes dilate.
   (6) Pulse slows and weakens, and breathing slows.
   (7) Victim lapses into unconsciousness.
d. Treatment:
   (1) Get victim out of the wind and weather.
   (2) Remove victim's clothing and get into a sleeping bag unclothed with him. Body heat is more readily transferred through flesh to flesh contact. Canteen(s) of hot water shielded with a T-shirt can be placed in the bag. Enveloping the head inside the bag for brief periods and breathing or blowing the warm breath will rapidly increase the bag temperature.
   (3) Prepare a fire and heat reflector.
   (4) Give hot drinks.
   (5) If breathing is imperceptible or stopped, give artificial respiration.
   (6) Get medical help.

e. Prevention:
Those most susceptible to hypothermia are generally suffering from the elements of exhaustion: inadequate or improper diet, not enough rest and too much physical exertion. Suffice to say, maintaining body heat and restricting heat losses will prevent hypothermia.

12. Snowblindness

a. Definition:
Inflammation and painful sensitiveness of the eyes with subsequent loss of vision.

b. Cause:
Burn on eye cornea caused by intense ultraviolet radiation which is generated by the sun and reflected from the surface of snow and ice.

c. Symptoms:
(1) Eyes feel scratchy, often with a burning sensation.
(2) More tearing than usual.
(3) Eyes sensitive to light.
(4) Halos seen around lights.
(5) Headaches.
(6) Loss of vision.

d. Treatment:
(1) Isolate the eyes from all light using bandage or any material which will accomplish this.
(2) Cold compresses and aspirin will help control pain.
(3) Treatment should begin with first detection.
(4) Most cases respond and recover within eighteen hours.
(5) Susceptibility increases after first incidence of snowblindness.

e. Prevention:
Wear snow goggles in snow country. If dark glasses are unavailable, soot can be applied to the inside of regular prescription eyeglass lenses. Snow goggles can be improvised from bark, wood, or cardboard by taking a piece of material as long as the head is wide and two or three inches deep, and cutting slits for

the eyes and an arc for the nose. Apply soot or charcoal to the inside of the material and tie it onto the head. Don't wait for discomfort before using goggles.

Bites and Stings

Among nature's myriad object lessons, the human encounter with poisonous reptiles and insects can be among the most memorable. Almost always the human who is wounded by one of these creatures is the human who is in the role of aggressor, even though he may only have been turning over rocks in his search of food or picking up bits of tinder from around an old tree stump.

Snakes, scorpions, and bees will very rarely attack unless provoked to do so. Playing with snakes, forgetting that a scorpion may have chosen a shoe in which to spend the night, or swatting at a bee are excellent subscriptions to the hard school of the wilderness. An easier way to go is to realize, and constantly be aware of, the nature of these creatures, and to exercise the cautions demanded by the situation. If you have to kill a snake for food, then kill it quickly and cleanly; otherwise, leave it alone. Watch where you put your hands and feet; if you have to turn over rocks for food or bait, do so with appropriate caution. Shake out your sleeping gear and clothing before using them while in scorpion country. Leave bees alone and let beekeepers do the honey collecting.

Ticks and mosquitoes present a different problem since they feed on the blood of mammals and need no provoking to do so.

13. Snakebite

The poisonous snakes of North America are the coral snakes and the pit vipers, which include the rattlesnake, the copperhead, and the water moccasin.

The Sonoran coral snakes, found in certain areas of the Southwest, especially Arizona, are easily identified by their adjacent red and yellow bands. These are not to be confused with king snakes which are non-poisonous and carry adjacent red and black bands. Sonoran coral snakes are small, so small that they can bite only fingers, toes, folds of skin, and such. These snakes cannot strike and retreat, but must hang on and chew.

Pit vipers are named for the heat-sensing pit carried between the nostril and the eye and can also be recognized by the single scales which extend beneath the body behind the anal plate. Non-poisonous snakes carry two or so sets of double scales in that area. See Figure.

Toxins from a poisonous snakebite travel through the lymph system, and treatment involves retarding the flow of lymph so that the toxin is allowed to spread very slowly, and thus is diluted by the body so that none but the area of the bite is subjected to a high toxin concentration. The only alternative to this is treatment with antivenin which will neutralize the venom.

Some facts concerning poisonous snake bites:

1. In 25 percent of snake bite cases **no** venom is transmitted.
2. In another 25% **little** venom is transmitted.
3. 70 percent of snake bites occur at or near the ankle.

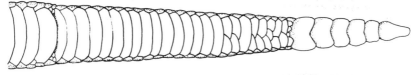

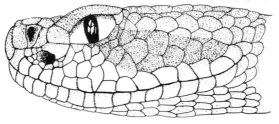

4. 85 percent of **untreated** bite victims survive.
5. 99 percent of **treated** bite victims survive.
a. Symptoms: (Poisonous)
   (1) Usually two small puncture marks in skin with additional rows of scratches caused by smaller teeth behind fangs.
   (2) Intense burning pain within one minute when bitten by a pit viper; pain not as intense and a little longer in coming if bitten by a coral snake.
   (3) Local swelling may obscure puncture marks.
   (4) Area around bite discolors to purple or green.
   (5) Feeling of dryness in mouth.
aa. Symptoms: (Non-poisonous)
   (1) Usually leaves two U-shaped rows of fine tooth marks.
   (2) Little pain or swelling.
b. Treatment: (Poisonous)
   (1) Inject antivenin as soon as possible to neutralize the venom. More than one injection will probably be required. The smaller the individual's size, the greater the requirement for additional injection. If the individual is allergic to antivenin, the amount given does not increase the allergic reaction. (Snakebite kits containing antivenin, instruments, and instructions can be purchased through pharmacies, and occasionally rented on a returnable basis from pharmacies in snake infested regions.) If antivenin is unavailable, if no trained medic is present, and if medical treatment or a hospital is more than 2½ to 3 hours away, the following steps should be taken:
   (2) Calm the victim.
   (3) Apply a constriction band between the heart and the bite to retard the flow of lymph through which the toxin spreads. Enough slack must be permitted to allow a finger to be pushed between the skin and the band. Pulse should be present on both sides of the constrictor.
   (4) Although the incision / suction method is effective in removing some of the venom, we do not recommend this procedure be implemented by the untrained. Three important things to remember if this procedure is used:

(a) The incision should be made longitudinally (parallel with the limb or appendage).

(b) Avoid incisions near veins, joints, and pulse points.

(c) Cover with sterile dressing and antibiotic ointment.

In the case of poisonous snakebites do not administer alcohol or stimulants. Alcohol taken internally serves to increase the rate at which the toxin will spread throughout the body and thus counteracts more beneficial treatment. It would be best to use the whiskey for cleaning the wound, saving some with which to celebrate recovery.

bb. Treatment: (Non-poisonous)

Clean wound with mild soap and water.

c. Prevention:

Wear calf-high boots in snake country; probe brush with walking stick before setting foot.

14. Tick Bite

The tick is a rather innocent appearing brown insect with a hard shell and is usually no larger than the head of a match. It is its habit to burrow, pointed head first, into the flesh of a mammal, thereby to sup on blood. The resultant infection, if any, is easy enough to treat. The danger comes when the tick is carrying Rocky Mountain spotted fever, tularemia, or relapsing fever. Since there is very little one can do about the disease without the aid of refined drugs, only the treatment as it pertains to tick removal will be discussed.

a. Treatment:

(1) Do not try to remove tick with unprotected fingers.

(2) Coat embedded tick with petroleum jelly, grease, or nail polish if available, or use antibacterial ointment and remove carefully with tweezers. If tweezers are not available, use a needle to gently pry tick from skin being careful not to crush the insect.

b. Prevention:

Wear high shoes with trouser leg ends tied around tops when hiking in tick infested country.

15. Bee Stings

With the exception of those who are allergic to bee stings or those who suffer a great number of stings within a few minutes, there is little to worry about after receiving a bee sting other than removing the stinger if it remains in the skin.

    a. Treatment:

        (1) Remove the stinger with an outward scraping motion of a fingernail, knife blade, or needle. Do not pinch the stinger between fingernails or tweezers. This action will force more venom out.

        (2) Wash area and apply antibacterial ointment.

16. Poisons (Internal, Plant Caused)

When identification of the poisonous plant is positive, refer to the treatment section for the plant in question in the Poisonous Plant section of this field guide.

Below is a list of treatments in order of priority for internal poisoning resulting from eating the toxic parts of the poisonous plants described in the manual.

    a. If the victim is conscious, have him drink large quantities of liquid. This serves to dilute the toxicity of the poison and should be done as quickly as possible after the poisoning.

    b. If the victim is conscious, induce vomiting by sticking a finger down the throat. This procedure should immediately follow the drinking of liquids as it is designed to expel the now diluted toxins from the digestive system.

    c. Repeat the above two steps several times, first inducing liquids, then vomiting, in order to expel as much of the toxins from the system as possible.

    d. After a thorough repetition of the liquid-vomit cycle, recheck the discussion of the plant and its toxins. Indicated for treating some plant poisonings is the ingestion of charcoal (activated). A few tablespoons of the powdered charcoal should be sufficient. Powdered activated charcoal, which absorbs certain toxins, can be obtained by pulverizing the charcoal found in your fire pit.

    e. Keep the patient comfortable. Keep him drinking more liquids than usual. Treat symptoms as they occur. Increase the intake of Vitamin C. This vitamin is believed to be effective in carrying toxins from the blood stream, ultimately dispelling them into the urine. Vitamin C can be obtained from the hips of the Wild Rose *(Rosa canina)*, from Pine needles *(Pinus),* and from the leaves of the Ground Ivy *(Glechoma hederacea).* These plant parts can be mashed, boiled, and strained through cloth to produce a "tea."

If the patient is unconscious, do not attempt to induce liquids or vomiting. Keep the patient warm and watch for signs of respiratory failure. Mouth-to-mouth artificial respiration is the most effective and can be rendered at any time should the patient need it, first by making certain that the mouth and throat are clear of obstructions.

If medical help is anticipated, preserve a sample of the offending plant for positive identification.

Time is an essential factor in many cases of internal poisoning. The patient generally can expect to survive the poisoning, but to feel sick for awhile. Care should be taken not to alarm or excite the patient unduly about the prospects of survival, and supportive treatment should be continued until after the patient feels well.

WHEN ALL ELSE FAILS

Death is not a popular subject. Living is. Although the primary thrust of this book is dedicated to the preservation of human life, the information contained herein is of only temporal value. It may extend your life by some brief, indeterminate period — but ultimately physical life will end.

Living, on the other hand, is a most popular subject, that is, providing the discussion of the subject deals with the here and now. Injection of anything of a spiritual nature which concerns eternal verities and consequences generally clouds this otherwise sunny subject.

It would be thought that guidance with respect to finding the accurate information which will lead to eternal life would be at least as aggressively sought after as the accurate information which leads to the sustaining of this life. The reader will heed this manual's advice pertaining to the eating of poison hemlock — but will the reader heed the advice from an authority far more commanding than this book, pronouncing that Christ came to give life and to give it abundantly and eternally.

Perhaps it may come as somewhat of a surprise to learn that the preservation of physical life is neither the loftiest consideration or the most important goal in creation. This then suggests that maybe there is something far greater in worth and importance than the preservation of human life.

NATURE BOUND began with the opening lines from a remarkable poem written by a sixteen year old boy. The title of this poem, *Thanatopsis,* is a Greek word which literally means "a view of death" — indeed, a strange way to begin a book about living and surviving. Careful study of this poem reveals a profound truth — a truth rarely discovered, even by men of great wisdom and maturity — that *death can be the doorway to life.*

I cannot tell you that William Cullen Bryant, as that sixteen year old boy, fully understood this truth, nor can I tell you that he intended the deeper Biblical implications of this truth. However, he knew that life does, in fact, exist beyond the grave.

Whereas *Thanatopsis* deals with truth from a more temporal and human point of view, the Bible sets forth this marvelous truth from God's perspective — dealing with spiritual and eternal verities. The mortal mind considers death a great mystery and much to be feared. Mortal eyes cannot perceive the magnitude, majesty and dimension of the unseen. But that does not alter its reality.

So then, how is death a doorway to life?

In the New Testament a despised Galilean carpenter said, "Most assuredly, I say to you, he who hears My word and believes in Him who sent me has everlasting life, and shall not come into judgment, *but has passed from death into life.*" John 5:24 NKJ.

Clearly Jesus is here talking about something other than physical life. The fact is, that we can conclude from this statement that one can be dead without having died and living without possessing "real" life!

Now death from the human perspective is the cessation of all vital signs. Death from God's perspective occurs at the moment of the first unrighteous thought or action. Here death is viewed from its most tragic and ultimate state — separation from God. Romans 5:12 NKJ states, "Therefore, just as through one man (Adam) sin entered the world, and *death through sin,* and thus *death spread to all men, because all sinned* —. Hence, apart from Christ, we are the living dead.

Christ taught, "I am the way, the truth, and the life." John 14:6. We can conclude from this statement that to alter the condition of being among the living dead, some sort of "new" life must come from Christ.

But how does this occur?

Jesus, in speaking to a respected leader who had come to him in the night said, "For God so loved the world that he gave his only begotten Son, that whoever believes in Him should not perish but have everlasting life." John 3:16 NKJ.

Yes, it is just that uncomplicated. Jesus came to give life where death reigns — to give it abundantly and eternally. Here then is a life which transcends death, a life made possible by and through the doorway of death.

APPENDIX – SURVIVAL AND FIRST AID GEAR

The length of your wilderness stay, time of year, type of environment and mode of travel all have an influence on what survival and first aid gear should be included. Adequate clothing and a quality hunting knife and stone, are essential. In addition to these your survival kit should include the following as an absolute minimum:

Compass: There is a wide range of types and prices, but the important consideration is the ability to read it and orient a map with it. For these reasons I recommend that the compass be of a size that is 360 degrees marked and easily read.

Whistle: It takes much less energy to blow a whistle than to shout. A police type whistle made of durable plastic and with a lanyard attached is best. In sub-freezing temperatures a metal whistle set between moist lips can freeze against the lips and is therefore unacceptable.

Matches and Match Container: 15-20 matches should be of the strike-anywhere stick type and coated with a varnish or other waterproofing agent. Cylindrical plastic match containers with a screw cap and striker provide additional match protection.

Candle: The four to six inch plumber's candle has far greater life than a match; hence, a simple rule should be followed: matches are to light candles.

Surgical Tubing: This may seem like a strange item to put in a survival kit, but it is a real must. Among other applications it is excellent for sling shot rubber, can be used in traps and snares, and makes a straw for sucking water from the collecting container in the bottom of a solar still.

Fly Line: Although any fly line will work, tapered line is preferable.

Fishing Flies: These five flies will catch fish nearly anywhere in the world: black gnat, royal coachman, gray hackle, brown hackle, and mosquito.

Monofilament Line: A small spool of four to six pound test is adequate.

Safety Pins: Three safety pins approximately 1½ inches in length work well as eyes for a primitive fishing pole (39.1).

Copper Wire: Several feet of fairly lightweight annealed copper wire is excellent for making snares (35.1).

Also Recommended Survival Items:

Signal Mirror: A metal mirror approximately 4 x 4 inches with both sides reflective and a hole 5/16 inch in diameter in the mirror center.

Fire Start Tablets: Although the candle is normally sufficient, a fire starting tablet will burn for five to seven minutes and, unlike the candle, a fire can be built directly over it.

Aluminum Foil: A one-ounce sheet of heavy-duty foil will provide everything from a heat reflector to a cooking pot.

Water Purification Tablets: Normally sold in a tiny bottle. Use per instruction label.

Plastic Sheeting: Approximately one mil and a minimum of six feet square.

First Aid Items:

Gauze pads (4) (4 x 4"): For direct application over larger wounds and for use when bleeding must be controlled by direct pressure against the wound.

Adhesive strips (4) (1"): For small cuts, blisters and abrasions.

Adhesive tape roll (1) (½"): For holding gauze pads in place and for many other emergency field uses.

Butterfly bandages (2) medium: For pulling together the skin of slash type wounds until stitches can be inserted.

Antiseptic swabs (2) (medium): For cleaning wound area, sterilizing needle, etc. Pads containing at least 50% alcohol are suggested.

Antibacterial ointment: My preference is for the 1/32 ounce size (sampler size) of Neosporin®. This particular ointment is highly effective for a variety of wounds, yet is easily thawed if it becomes frozen. Whatever brand you select, it should not be readily affected by either freezing or very warm temperatures, and non-toxic to the eyes.

Aspirin (12) (5 grain tablets): Assists in control of headache, minor pain and fever. Dosage: one or two tablets with water, if available, every four hours.

Salt tablets (12): Per instructions on container label.

Sewing needle: Splinters and thorns may be exposed and removed with the needle.

GLOSSARY OF PLANT TERMS

Acrid: Sharp and harsh or unpleasant, pungent in taste or odor.
Aesthetic: Beautiful, sensitive to beauty.
Alkaloid: Colorless, bitter organic material.
Alternate: Not opposite as in the case of leaves on a stem.
Annual: A plant which matures and dies within one year.
Annulus: A part, structure, or marking resembling a ring.
Aril: An exterior covering or appendage of a class of seeds.
Aromatic: Having a strong or distinctive smell.
Astringent: Causing to shrink or contract.
Axil: The angle formed between a leaf and stem.
Axis: Point of central support.
Basal: Located at or near the base.
Biennial: A plant which matures and dies within two years.
Branchlet: A small branch, a smaller branch growing from a larger one.
Bract: A reduced leaf or modified leaf extending under a flower or flower cluster.
Bristle: A short, stiff, coarse hair or filament.
Bulb: Plant part, generally underground, used by the plant for food storage and propagation.
Capsule: A closed receptacle containing spores or seeds.
Cathartic: That which cleanses or makes free of an unwanted substance.
Cleft: Cut halfway or nearly to middle.
Compound: Consisting of two or more similar parts (i.e. leaf divided into leaflets).
Conic: Resembling a cone in shape.
Conical: Cone-shaped.
Coniferous: Bearing cones.
Convex: Arched up, bulging out.
Corm: Enlarged fleshy stem base, bulb-like but solid.

CPR: Cardiopulmonary resuscitation.

Crenate: Having a margin cut into rounded scallops.

Deciduous: Leaf-bearing tree or plant which loses foliage at the end of its growing season.

Dentate: Having teeth or pointed conical projections.

Dermatitis: Inflammation of the skin.

Drupelet: Small, individual, seed-bearing fruit often combined in groups (e.g., a blackberry is a mass of drupelets).

Elliptical: Oval with both ends alike.

Elongated: Long in proportion to width.

Emetic: That which causes vomiting.

Evergreen: Bearing foliage throughout the year.

Fetid: Having a heavy offensive smell.

Fibrous: Consisting of fibers.

Fiddlehead: Curved like a violin head.

Follicle: A seed vessel or fruit that splits along one seam only.

Genus: Plant family subdivision which includes one or more species.

Glaborous: Without hairs or projections, smooth.

Glandular: Containing glands (secreting organs within plant structure).

Herb: Seed plant in which stem dies back after one season's growth.

Herbaceous: Having the characteristics of a herb, having little or no woody tissue.

Hybridize: To produce a cross between two species.

Keeled: Having a pronounced ridge in a leaf or stem.

Lance-like: Narrow, broadest at base and gradually tapering at loose end.

Lanceolate: Shaped like a lance head; tapering to a point at the apex end and occasionally at the base.

Lateral veins: Veins on, directed toward, or coming from the side.

Leaflet: Leaf-like division of a compound leaf.

Leafstalk: Slender stem which supports a leaf.

Legume: The fruit or seed of leguminous plants (i.e., peas, beans).

Linear: Long, narrow (e.g. grass-like).
Lobe: A rounded projecting part.
Longitudinal: Relating to the length.
Margin: The edge of a leaf or other plant organ.
Membraneous: Thin, pliable (freely bending) and often somewhat transparent.
Mottled: Having colored spots or blotches.
Obcordate: Heart-shaped with attachment (stem, stalk) at the pointed end.
Oblong: Longer than broad, elongated.
Obovate: Inversely ovate with broader top end.
Obtuse: Blunted or not pointed.
Orbicular: Round, circular.
Oval: Broadly elliptical, egg-shaped.
Ovate: Egg-shaped with broader basal end.
Palmate: Having veins or lobes radiating from a common point.
Panicle: Pyramid-shaped, loosely branched flower cluster.
Paniculate: Having the characteristics of a panicle.
Parasitic: A plant that lives in or on another plant.
Pemmican: Concentrated food used by North American Indians consisting of lean meat (pounded fine), and mixed with melted fat. Frequently berries and occasionally nuts were included.
Perennial: Plant which lives and fruits three or more years.
Petioled: Having a slender stalk by which a leaf is attached to the stem.
Piedmont: Area at mountain base.
Pinnate: Having similar parts arranged on opposite sides of an axis.
Pinnatifid: Divided in a pinnate manner.
Pith: Soft, spongy material in stem or root center.
Pollen: A mass of microspores in a seed plant, appearing usually as fine dust.
Potherb: Herb, the leaves or stems of which are boiled for eating or used as a flavoring.
Poultice: Hot, soft, moist mass applied to a sore or inflamed body part.

Raceme: Simple flower cluster having its flowers on nearly equal stalks along a stem.

Rhizomatous: Having or resembling a rhizome.

Rhizome: Underground plant stem, usually horizontal, producing shoots above and roots below; sometimes called rootstalk.

Rootstalk (Rootstock): Underground plant source (rhizome).

Rosette: Radiating basal leaf cluster which is shaped like a rose.

Scaly: A series of thin, flake-like scales.

Saccate: Having the form of a sac or pouch.

Sepal: One of the leaf-like divisions of the outer covering of a flower, usually green.

Sessile: Without a stalk, attached directly by the base.

Sheath: Leaf part surrounding the stem.

Shrub: Woody, generally multi-stemmed plant; bush.

Silica: Hard, glassy material.

Sori (Sorus): A cluster of sporangia (reproductive bodies) in ferns.

Species: Distinct kind of plant within a genus.

Spike: Flower cluster with flowers borne along a stem.

Spores: Mostly single-celled organisms capable of reproducing new plants.

Style: Slender upper part of the plant ovary.

Succulent: Fleshy.

Tannin: An acid, yellowish, astringent used in tanning, dyeing, medicine, etc.

Taproot: Main root, generally vertical, which is the underground extension of the stem.

Tendril: Threadlike part of a climbing plant that attaches itself to something to support the plant.

Ternate: Arranged in threes.

Trifoliate: Possessing three leaves or leaflets.

Tripinnate: Twice pinnate or bipinnate with each division pinnate (see pinnate).

Tuber: The thickened portion of an underground stem (i.e., rootstalk).

Tufted: Closely or tightly clustered.

Twiner: A plant which achieves support by twining.

Umbel: An umbrella or flattopped flower cluster in which the flowers appear to spring from the same point.

Umbellet (Umbellule): A secondary umbel in a compound umbel.

Volva: A membranous covering that encloses the base of many fungi, especially mushrooms.

Whorled: Three or more similar flowers or leaves radiating from a more or less distinct joint of a stem.

Winnow: To remove the chaff (unwanted seed coverings and debris) from the seed by exposing to air current — normally by gently tossing in the air.

EDIBLE PLANT INDEX
Alphabetic Common

Alphabetic Scientific

POISONOUS PLANT INDEX

Alphabetic Common

Alphabetic Scientific